SERVICE VIRTUALIZATION

REALITY IS OVERRATED

John Michelsen
Jason English

technologies
PRESS

Apress®

Service Virtualization: Reality Is Overrated

President and Publisher: Paul Manning
Acquisitions Editor: Robert Hutchinson
Technical Reviewer: Ruston Vickers
Editorial Board: Steve Anglin, Mark Beckner, Ewan Buckingham, Gary Cornell,
    Morgan Ertel, Jonathan Gennick, Jonathan Hassell, Robert Hutchinson,
    Michelle Lowman, James Markham, Matthew Moodie, Jeff Olson, Jeffrey
    Pepper, Douglas Pundick, Ben Renow-Clarke, Dominic Shakeshaft, Gwenan
    Spearing, Matt Wade, Tom Welsh
Coordinating Editor: Rita Fernando
Copy Editor: Jennifer Sharpe
Compositor: Bytheway Publishing Services
Indexer: SPi Global
Cover Designer: Anna Ishchenko

Distributed to the book trade worldwide by Springer-Verlag New York, Inc., 233 Spring
Street, 6th Floor, New York, NY 10013. Phone 1-800-SPRINGER, fax 201-348-4505,
e-mail orders-ny@springer-sbm.com, or visit www.springeronline.com.

For information on translations, please contact us by e-mail at info@apress.com, or
visit www.apress.com.

Apress and friends of ED books may be purchased in bulk for academic, corporate, or
promotional use. eBook versions and licenses are also available for most titles. For
more information, reference our Special Bulk Sales–eBook Licensing web page at
www.apress.com/bulk-sales. To place an order, email your request to support@apress.
com.

Contents

About the Authors

John Michelsen, CTO, CA Technologies and Co-Founder, ITKO

John has lived his career helping enterprise customers push the leading edge of IT transformation to deliver on business outcomes and is a highly respected technologist who moves others to action. As the CTO of CA Technologies, John is responsible for technical leadership and innovation, as well as aligning CA's software strategy, architecture, and partner relationships to deliver customer value. With 12 patents awarded or in process and with market-leading inventions delivered in database, distributed computing, virtual/cloud management, multichannel web application portals, Service Virtualization (LISA®), and many other areas, John is a factory of innovation.

John is a frequent writer in leading trade publications and has presented at technology and business conferences around the world. He joined CA Technologies in 2011 through its acquisition of ITKO, a company he co-founded and drove successfully for 12 years. Prior to ITKO, John's broad technology experience included leading SaaS and e-commerce transformations for global enterprises at Trilogy and Agency.com. In his spare time, he enjoys vacationing with his family on islands or in the mountains, and he has also become an expert at country and Texas swing dancing.

Jason English, CA Technologies Director, Product Marketing and ITKO Historian

Jason joined ITKO (now a CA Technologies company) in 2004 as employee #3, functioning as the company's "Marketing Department" during many stretches of its existence, while handling other tasks from software UI design to sales support.

Before managing marketing for ITKO, Jason was Executive Producer of the in2action interactive consulting unit at i2 Technologies, where he was responsible for web marketing and messaging during a period of extreme growth, as well as working directly with major companies of every industry to build easy-to-use workflows for complex B2B collaboration systems. Prior to that, he served as one of the first information architects, defining customer experience for Fortune 500 clients at the pioneering interactive firm Agency. com. He has also designed, written, and scored soundtracks for internationally released computer games in addition to producing advertising and television commercials. He continues to compose and play music and remains an active brewer.

About the Technical Reviewer

Ruston Vickers, CA Technologies VP Research and Development and ITKO Co-Founder

As co-founder of ITKO (now a CA Technologies company) and leader of R&D efforts, Ruston has been instrumental in advancing the company's product suite from its inception. He manages all customer product deployments and is the lead developer of CA LISA's integration frameworks, which help clients gain tremendous extensibility and quality across many technologies within complex IT environments.

Prior to ITKO, Ruston designed and built solutions for world-class clients in energy, automotive, and travel industries while working at Agency.com and EDS. Early in his career, he developed some of the first highly interactive online experiences for EDS, General Motors, and Dr. Martens. He also worked closely with Netscape and Macromedia during development of new technologies for dynamic and streaming content delivery. Ruston is also an aficionado of high-end guitar and sound gear, which generally gets him VIP access to all entrances. He holds a Bachelor of Science degree from Texas Tech University.

Acknowledgments

The authors would like to thank:

Our patient wives, impatient kids, Moms, Dads, and families;

The visionary customers from whom John has learned so much, for your help documenting dozens of great SV examples and case studies with Jason over the past six years, especially Sven Gerjets, Laura Miller, Russ Wheaton, Jamie Williams, and many others for allowing us to recount your stories herein;

All the genius, committed technologists from ITKO's early days who made this incredible new technology happen, especially our cofounder Ruston Vickers—you are all the best in the business;

Ken Ahrens and Rajeev Gupta for helping us kill it on a couple of the tougher sections on SV process and performance techniques;

Shridhar Mittal, Chris Kraus, Anuj Gulati, and Luther Birdzell for valuable input and help;

Robert Humphrey for championing the cause, and Scott King, Paul Neumann, Jim Dugger, Justin Vaughan-Brown, and everyone else who stepped up while Jason was off noodling on this book;

And finally, all the technologists, executives, and partners who are acting on this unique opportunity to make a game-changing new approach real for business. We hope this book inspires you to take it even further.

Virtually There at FedEx®

It's a Reality Most Businesses Would Want to Run Away From

Fifteen years ago, a team at FedEx had to make absolutely, positively certain that their deliveries would be supported by a software architecture of around 200 systems. Today, the number of moving parts and services they must fit together *easily exceeds several thousand unique IT services and systems*. And that's just one key group. Millions of end-customer and partner transactions hit FedEx systems from around the globe every day.

Here's what Russ Wheaton—Director IT, FedEx—had to say about their journey:

> In keeping with the customer demand and expectation of the times, our company was testing a very specific stack of software 15–18 years ago, with some of our key systems originally having been built in the '80s. The earliest goal was to certify software functions that were considered "revenue-impacting" or "customer-facing" to our business. As time progressed and the system reality came closer to business expectation, the number, type and scale of the systems falling into this category grew quite a bit.

> We were facing a challenge: As we continued to roll out and connect more services to provide a higher degree of flexibility and service level to our customers, many more core systems were playing in the space of customer or revenue impacting. As the number of interconnected systems rose, the complexity of the "business transaction" increased

significantly. This, combined with a fast-growing company strategy realizing ever-increasing shipping transactions, forced a big think on how we would address the end-to-end certification of the core flow, without regularly adding resources or budget to make it happen. We needed to change our strategy.

Around the same time, a new movement was growing called SOA (Service-Oriented Architecture) which promised to simplify the problem via a set of principles and methodologies targeting the design of discrete but interoperable services. This was great in that it gave us more reuse and faster development of common enterprise services, allowing us to design, deploy, and decouple at a much more manageable level, eliminating many of the "big-system" dependencies and the fall-forward strategy.

But there was a downside that SOA introduced for the large system certification processes. When you have a lot of teams or systems depending on one another being ready, that dependency has an impact on schedules. If the services needed at a specific time in the certification process weren't all sized appropriately, or were not ready to go, or were coming together for the first time in end-to-end testing, it just didn't work. It became an exercise in heroics to bring the pieces together while staying on schedule.

About seven years ago or so, we introduced interface standardization as a core architecture principle that would sit across all our development silos. We decided to standardize interface technology on both the transport and encoding. Many good things resulted from having well-defined (even in some cases self-defining) interfaces that helped significantly with software design and delivery in a complex heterogeneous environment. We had also hoped that we were making an investment in our future thinking that someday this would facilitate a more standard, repeatable certification process for our very complex applications. Ideally we could leverage a "simulation" technology (other industries had been leveraging simulators for decades), where we could stand up analogs of our well-defined interface and simulate them for functional or performance testing purposes in such a way that dependent development teams could work independently of one another from a development schedule perspective as long as the interface or "contract" between the two was well-defined and standardized.

While that was important for our schedule, we were also highly concerned with reliability. How could we certify each of these systems independently as a baseline and take a scientific approach, so that if one piece of code changed, we could ensure in an automated fashion that the results we expected were happening? In essence, could we leverage this technology to develop a new technique to push quality further up in the development lifecycle potentially as far as code and unit test?

For a company our size, the solutions we deploy to certify our revenue-impacting or customer-facing applications have to be technology-agnostic on the back end. We continue to work with the architect community to leverage standardized technologies like SOAP, REST, EJBs and integration buses, regardless of whether they talk to back-end mainframes, internal distributed services, clouds, or even external services. We know nirvana for us is to achieve consistent technology and encoding across all core enterprise interfaces.

Twenty years ago things were simpler. Business and IT were separated by a great divide. IT enabled things like accounting, but very little of the business productivity was driven by IT. But the Internet started bringing that gap together, and now business strategies are tied at the hip and very dependent upon the IT solutions and enabling strategies.

That puts pressure on our IT systems to look more like business solutions. We need IT to drive new capabilities, enable faster turnaround times for new services, and create greater agility for the business. We have to certify faster to get to market faster. And while IT evolves, customer expectations increase, and customer tolerance for system failure drops. Over time, in some cases, it has evolved from simply irritating the customer to impacting the customer's very business model.

We need to keep raising the bar on ourselves. If our systems are not fast, secure, and accurate, customers will do business elsewhere.

When John Michelsen was in our office a couple years ago, that was the situation I laid out for him: Ever-increasing business complexity and demand for new feature development, on time, right the first time, every time—while nobody gets any extra time, money, or resources to make it happen. We wanted to change the game to get more productivity out of the hours and people we had to meet that demand, while maintaining a sensible and rewarding work–life balance for our professionals. It is forcing us to rethink our environment.

Today, everything has gone virtual, giving us a higher degree of repeatability and predictability amongst other things. We have virtualized servers; the industry nailed that one years ago. Via Service-Oriented Architecture (SOA), commoditized services and data are commonplace in today's enterprise computing environment. With the introduction of Service Virtualization technologies, something we internally call

"Interface Simulation," we're now able to stand up hundreds of interfaces and virtual back ends without requiring the complex interdependencies of the peripheral systems (to the system under test). In one example from my team, we simulate 25 back-end services representing about 200 different servers in a space we traditionally struggled with. Interestingly enough, we didn't even test those services. We just needed them to test the higher-end dependent service, yet they took the bulk of the time to set up and administer.

Taking away the need to work with real systems has greatly simplified our process. For adoption, we had to prove that virtual services worked better than the real thing to gain trust. The first time we were able to hand a performance manager an extra week of time in his cycle, it was like giving him a sack of gold.

But acceptance of any change in mindset across an organization can be hard, especially when you are confronted with "the way it's always worked." So my advice to anyone considering moving to virtualized services and interfaces would be this: ***Pick a spot where you have the toughest constraints, focus on it, make it excellent***—and people will come out of the woodwork to support it.

Introduction

Whether you realize it or not, you are likely already in the business of making software. Service Virtualization is not just a topic for a select few IT professionals. If you are in a company that delivers services to customers over the Internet or enables sales and service teams through software, this book is for you.

Success is there for the faking. Service Virtualization offers a transformational new way to overcome the constraints that inhibit your teams from delivering software to production so you can get your company's products and services to market faster, better, and cheaper than your competition.

Service Virtualization Defined

Service Virtualization (SV) is the practice of capturing and simulating the behavior, data, and performance characteristics of dependent systems and deploying a Virtual Service that represents the dependent system without any constraints, thus allowing software to be developed and delivered faster, with lower costs and higher reliability. This rather concise definition of SV will be elaborated upon and refined in Chapter 5.

Service Virtualization includes a new type of technology and an accompanying methodology for "virtualizing everything" in the environment around any software-enabled or Internet-based business service or product you are developing. Since there are very few companies in business today that do not depend on software, the competitive and economic impact of Service Virtualization will be profound and far-reaching across many industries.

You Make the Transformation Happen

We will challenge you to understand your own role in advancing the transformational practice of Service Virtualization, whether you are an IT executive, delivery manager, architect, or in almost any way involved in software development. You will gain a basic understanding of how SV technology works to alleviate software constraints. More importantly, you will learn why, when, where, and how SV practices should be employed for maximum success and value to your business.

Practical applications for SV that are in use by enterprises today enable you to

- deliver faster

- reduce your infrastructure footprint

- transform your performance and scale

- manage your data scenarios

These are by no means the limit of what can be done with SV, but provide valuable approaches we have seen companies use to drastically reduce new feature delivery timelines, infrastructure, and labor costs, while eliminating unexpected risks from problematic software projects.

About This Book

This book assumes a basic understanding of how Internet-based business software projects are planned, budgeted, developed and delivered. The practice of Service Virtualization has profound potential for improving the time to market and overall competitiveness of any business strategy with a technology component. Organizational buy-in is key to success here, so while the core of Service Virtualization practitioners are software development, testing, and IT environments teams, we also focus on business-level approaches and benefits.

Disclosure: The writers of this book are a co-founder and early employee of the software firm ITKO, now a CA Technologies company. In 2007, ITKO invented, patented, and released the first Service Virtualization software on the market within their CA LISA® product suite. Now Service Virtualization is a growing category of software with established service provider offerings and related tools on the market from several leading vendors. This book's purpose is not to make claims about CA or LISA software products, but instead focuses on the best practices for enabling Service Virtualization practices, no matter what combination of tools you select and use in your environment.

Signposts in the Book

Look for these icons as you read—they'll highlight some useful supplemental information.

 Advice: These are tips that can help you smooth adoption of Service Virtualization practices for your business.

 Alert: These warnings can help you avoid common organizational pitfalls or implementation dangers often found to inhibit success.

 Geek Out: Engineers will find these details quite interesting, but if you are not reading for technical purposes, you may skip over these sections.

 Remember: Don't forget these points when embarking on your own implementation

Definitions: Terms of art are highlighted at first occurrence in the text with bold italics and an asterisk (**term***) and are defined in the Glossary.

The Business Imperatives: Innovate or Die

Almost all high-level enterprise executives when we first meet will say that software development is not really their core business. They'll say: "We are first and foremost driven to be leaders in the [banking-insurance-telco-utilities-retail-travel-health care] industry. Our core business is helping customers, not developing software." (Unless, of course, they are actually working for a software company.)

Well, we'd like to challenge that assumption right now. Any major company with an IT delivery component already has a huge software organization teeming under its surface, with thousands of developers, performance and test engineers, and support and customer representatives all attempting to drive technology to deliver on the expectations of the market. *I can't count how many CIOs go out of their way to tell me they have more developers on their staff than a software company the size of CA Technologies, or even in some cases Microsoft!*

Your enterprise software organization is likely spread out over multiple offices, organizational silos, and partners, and paid for out of multiple budgets—but it has a shared motivation: Innovate or die! Your competition has the same motivation too. This **innovation race** is driven by four very real business imperatives.

Consumers Have No Mercy

The ability to innovate and deliver new business capabilities for customers via IT is no longer just a perk for most companies—it is the critical factor for success. Innovative software that performs and works flawlessly for customers wherever and however they choose to interact with your company has now become a primary competitive differentiator.

Fail to deliver, and get left behind. Today's consumer has no patience for a poorly performing app and no tolerance for unexpected errors when doing business with your company.

Take my teenage daughter as an example of how much today's and tomorrow's customers expect from IT. I keep her equipped with a debit card for day-to-day purchases (I am also a bit of a pushover for my girl!). One day she happens to be in line at the food court in the mall and calls me to say she needs $10 in her account for lunch right now. I say, "OK, honey, let me see if the bank can transfer the funds that fast from my phone." She says, "Well if it can't, let's SWITCH BANKS."

Scary? Yes! Consumerization of IT means "no mercy" from today's customers. Had my bank not provided immediate access to those funds through my iPhone app, she would have been telling her 1,350 Facebook friends how awful my bank is and looking for a better one. They are accustomed to transacting business with your company wherever they are, whether online or on the phone, and getting almost instant gratification. If there's a problem with your application delivery, the competition is always just a click away.

Business Demands Agile Software Delivery

Let's take a look at one of the largest banks we have worked with. Rather than advertise their long history, strong asset base, deep professional experience, and many physical locations, they run television ads for things like:

- A new "quick pay" web service
- A new "scan checks from my phone" app
- A better security system for catching online identity theft

None of these above are traditional defining characteristics of a financial institution—these are all new software features that had better work as advertised when delivered in a web browser or smartphone! It just goes to show that the rapid design and development of software applications is now a primary way companies require us to go to market and differentiate in today's consumer-driven economy.

To top it off, over the last decade most major enterprises have put a huge emphasis on cutting IT costs as much as possible, and therefore the IT budgets of the old dot-com days aren't coming back. Do more with less. This is the **new normal*** state of IT economics that we must function in. The very same bank mentioned above is expected to take hundreds of millions of dollars out of their IT spend over the next few years. That means your business must be ready to deliver new software functionality at breakneck speed in an increasingly difficult environment, without an increasing budget expenditure to match.

Increased Change and Complexity Are Inevitable

In an attempt to make IT more agile in delivering new software features at Internet speed, most companies have moved toward composite application development approaches. These new service-oriented methodologies espoused the idea that new software could be produced more rapidly atop of existing systems when broken up into smaller functional units or "services" that were more reusable and loosely coupled.

While this approach did accelerate development on a functional unit basis at first, over time it also created a "spaghetti mess" of services architecture with highly unpredictable results: many interdependent components, developed using heterogeneous technologies, managed and owned by distributed teams, with each version changing on its own release cycle (Figure 2-1). Yesteryear's unitary "app" has evolved into a composite of several piece-parts of several other applications.

What happens in this type of highly volatile environment? We must account for this agile service development by expecting to discover more and more software errors occurring owing to the unintended consequences of change. Some IT shops are doing more break-fix in production than ever, which is not a sustainable model. Others throw more and more budget at each project, sometimes increasing their lab infrastructure and QA budgets by 5 or 10 times in an attempt to ensure the software will function as expected once released.

One major insurance payer we know said they routinely "planned for their unpredictability" (oh, the irony) in delivering software by automatically adding **30 percent more hours** to the end of every project plan!

Business Software Cannot Sustain without Simulation

If we built commercial airplanes the same way we build software today, we would never fly!

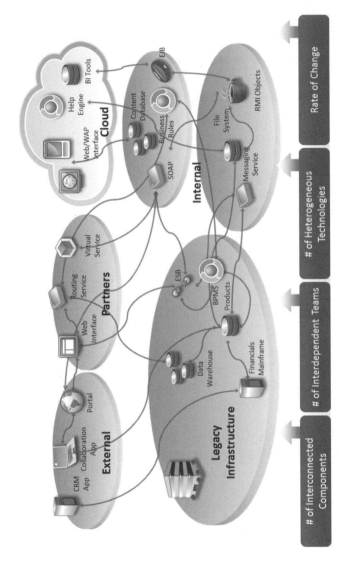

Figure 2-1. Composite application sprawl happens due to the decoupling of applications into service-based, distributed architectures, consisting of multiple interconnected heterogeneous technologies that are frequently changed and updated by multiple delivery teams.

Let's compare your business software development challenges to the manufacturing process for commercial airplanes. If we were the design team for a new wing and we performed that task as we build software today, we would demand hundreds of actual airplanes full of cargo and a pilot as our "lab." We would then crash hundreds of planes in our horribly inefficient and desperate attempt to get our new wing design to fly.

But that is exactly what we commonly see companies do with the critical software that runs their operations today! In software, if some component fails in production, we just *send the release back to development* and eat the cost of finding and fixing those errors, miss opportunities, and fail in front of customers.

You can see that if airplane manufacturers took this "wait and see, then send back to dev" approach, they'd go out of business long before we ever had viable commercial aircraft.

Today, aircraft design, manufacturing, and flight are the result of a process of constant simulation, testing, monitoring, and improvement. Each and every part of the plane's design is developed, then tested independently using modeling and simulation, and then tested again as part of an integrated system, while being continuously monitored in-flight for any performance issue. Real wing-design teams know that they don't need planes to build a wing: they need modeling tools and a wind tunnel.

Simulation tools utilize feedback from this real production data to ensure correctly functioning components without waiting until the integration stage for verification. Pilots must even spend hours training in flight simulators that virtualize the airplane's behavior in real-world scenarios, without the risk.

The design of an aircraft presents engineers with an extremely complex architecture of thousands of unique and highly interdependent components, systems, and sensors. It would be impossible to account for all of the "what-if" scenarios of introducing a new element to a real aircraft without simulation.

Think about it: You can't expect to find every environmental condition that our wing will face during a live test flight to see if it works—of course not! Instead, we must have complete control over the environment—a "wind tunnel" that simulates all the environmental conditions we need without the real plane. This allows us to fully verify the design much faster. *Simulation—it's just science, Einstein!*

Today's software architectures now look more like a complicated aircraft design than the previous simplistic **client/server*** or on-premise systems we once knew (Figure 2-2). It is surprising any business software runs at all given the woeful lack of robust simulation.

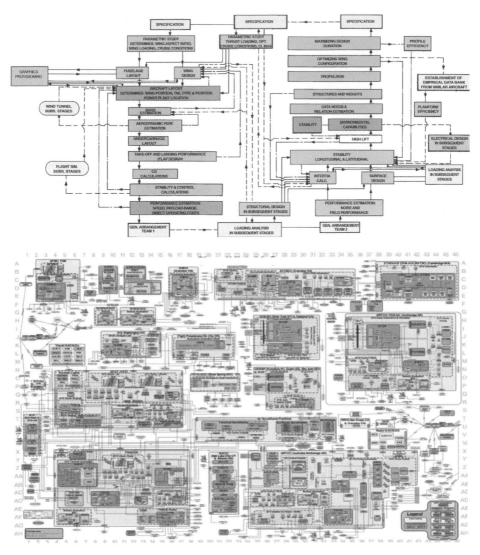

Figure 2-2. An aircraft design process (top) compared with a typical composite application architecture view (bottom) (US FAA NAS public network architecture, 2008)

Other industries—from consumer electronics to automotive to pharmaceuticals—understand the science of modeling and simulation for experimentation purposes in design and development. With so much critical functionality on the line, it is now time that the business software industry sign up for the same scientific discipline of proving out our hypotheses by simulating real-world environments ahead of delivery, for more predictable and safe results.

How We Got Here

Let's go back to the days of running a software shop twenty years ago—before many of today's developers had even compiled their first line of code. Grizzled techies still talk about it like the Golden Age of software engineering, but it was such a simple world compared to today.

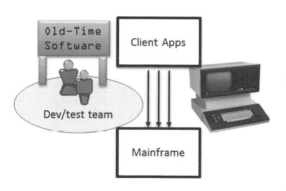

Software applications were essentially closed, monolithic systems. There was one client UI, the software ran on one target platform, and we usually had a year or more to get the project done. Better yet, everyone on the project was likely co-located in the same building and could have lunch together.

Yes, we had to homebrew many parts of the system to make it work. But in the early '90s, we had much lower expectations of interactivity or system intelligence. We had little or no interconnectivity or reliance on any external systems—everything was completely under our control. And we thought it was hard back then...

Things have gotten incredibly difficult since then. We now have an enormous distributed staff and many partners, under incredible pressure to deliver new business functionality faster, with an ever-increasing amount of complexity and change in IT environments.

From Monolithic to Composite Apps

It's not like anyone wanted to make applications evolve this way. Customers demanded higher levels of service to meet their specific needs. Therefore, companies started keeping track of more customer information, as well as offering more complex products and services that needed to be accounted for by those core *mainframes**.

Rather than replace these often irreplaceable systems, in the later '80s the rise of the desktop PC happened, and we naturally learned to "layer" on new technology and relational data to try and abstract new software features in these clients, thereby working atop the slow-changing nature of core servers.

To survive, businesses needed to become more flexible and develop new software to meet the needs of customers. So each evolution of our applications—from the still-often-critical mainframe to client/server and n-Tier apps to today's service-oriented composite apps (Figure 3-1)—was simply the next way to respond to ever-faster-changing customer and market demands with new software, while carrying forward the core systems the business relied upon. We frequently describe our customers' environments as "museums without plaques."

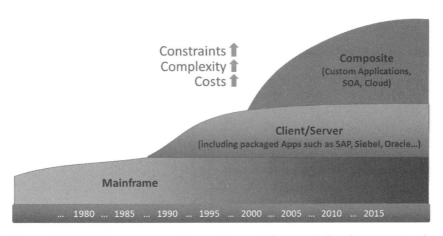

Figure 3-1. Evolution to composite apps from mainframe and client/server approaches. Note that the existing technology investments never go away.

Today's Complex Service Environments

Let's take a look at a simplified reference architecture for a modern composite application, which we will reference throughout this book (Figure 3-2). (If you are not a developer, don't worry. You will understand this!) A real enterprise software implementation will consist of many, many more boxes, but the basic concept is a multi-tiered "layer cake" that looks like this:

UI Layers

Services

Integration

Back ends

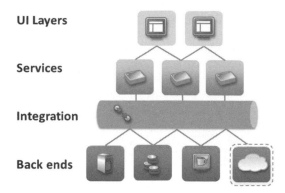

Figure 3-2. Simplified architecture diagram of a typical modern composite application with multiple tiers of technology.

UI Layers: End users interface with apps through web or device UI layers that usually contain very little business logic. These components are usually the most dynamic and variable aspects of an application, as any user experience may be customized and configured to accept a near-infinite number of possible scenarios.

Services: Web and UIs running on app servers call on underlying services layers, which are modular components that contain much of the discrete business functionality that development teams are building. These services basically process requests when called and pass along data using an appropriate message protocol (SOAP, XML, etc.). While there are industry standards around these protocols, companies inevitably have customized formats for some distributed communication.

Integration: As composite applications become more complex and new services and systems are constantly added, the orchestration of many moving parts must be addressed. To coordinate these services to meet the needs of robust business processes, most enterprises adopted an **Enterprise Application Integration (EAI)*** approach with an integration "backbone" or **Enterprise Service Bus (ESB)*** system as a broker to route and queue up messages from the services layer and make calls to the back-end mainframes and systems of record when needed.

Back Ends: Most requests of the top layer of the application will eventually delegate to these systems for execution. These are the core systems of record for a company such as SAP and Oracle Financials, as well as legacy applications and third-party hosted applications and mainframes. Software development teams usually try to minimize changes to these highly utilized environments as these layers handle important live tasks and are difficult or costly to change or replicate.

As you can see, each business function supported by a given UI will have many downstream steps of business logic, data, and dependencies that must respond in order to successfully execute a given business workflow.

Tech Note: While every composite app is unique, they usually share common design patterns. As you move outward from the core systems toward the surface of an architecture, you will notice that underlying back-end systems and data sources are generally slow-changing (requiring an "act of God" to make a major shift), middle-tiers are updated a little more frequently (new processes or integrations added), while new features are implemented most frequently and cause the most changes at the services and application UI layers.

From Waterfall to Agile Development

Let's take a look at the evolution of software development now through a process lens. Development teams are attempting to answer the need for speed as well—by moving away from the exhaustive **Waterfall*** development method of several sequential, gated steps that a team must finish and verify in order to complete a release (Figure 3-3).

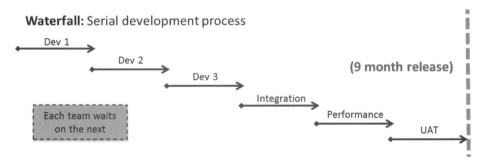

Figure 3-3. The Waterfall development process consists of several sequential development and test gates over time, building toward a long-term project release.

Instead of taking months or more to deliver a release using the Waterfall approach, in the last 15 years we have seen a huge surge in popularity for **Agile*** development methodologies. The Agile approach recommends smaller, independent teams to define, test, and develop small units of functionality in shorter cycles or **scrums*** with short-term deliverables or "sprints" toward the end goal (Figure 3-4).

One cool aspect of Agile is that it promotes **Test-Driven Development* (TDD)**—which means developers "Test, then Code." First, a test is written.

Agile: Faster iterations and releases

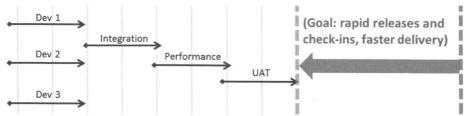

Figure 3-4. Agile development process breaks development into smaller, independent teams with the responsibility to develop smaller units of functionality in fast iterations or "scrums," with the goal of faster alignment to the delivery requirement than Waterfall approaches.

Then the developer starts coding. When the developed code passes the test, this is a proof point that the code works as intended. These unit tests are typically quite simple and test for the "happy path" of what the developer expects to deliver, but when developers unit test at a higher frequency, it increases the quality of each dev cycle. In this manner, incremental adjustments of software to meet a business requirement can be made over the course of several iterations, and the productivity (and engagement level) of development teams should be increased.

Agile development also lends itself naturally to service-oriented technology approaches, as smaller units of functionality can be built and reused in the environment as modular, decoupled components. Agile proved excellent for new, clean-slate development projects. For larger enterprises, however, it often failed to deliver the expected boost in successful release speed. The combination of distributed Agile development with service-based applications, atop a raft of existing system and data dependencies, soon created a new set of challenges that caused project delays and failures, in the form of **constraints**.*

 Tip on Agile: Tons of great developer-level content has been published about Agile. We recommend starting with "The Agile Manifesto" site at http://agilemanifesto.org and following up with books by some of the leading authors in that space.

 Caveat about Agile: Since most Agile authors largely focus on developer-level coding and testing activities, they tend to ignore the realities of interconnectedness and complexity inherent in enterprise IT. Therefore, at this time, Agile experts seldom acknowledge the external constraints and need for simulation that we are talking about here.

Constraints: The Enemy of Agility

Constraints are any dependencies that delay the completion of a task in the software development lifecycle that are not within the control of the team responsible for the task. Constraints are the primary reasons why business software projects are delivered late, over budget, and with poor quality.

Ask Bob the Development Manager why his team missed another delivery deadline, and you will never hear Bob say, *"It's because we're just not smart enough . . ."* or *"My team just isn't motivated enough . . ."* You will instead likely hear Bob rationalize the failure thusly:

"We did everything we could do. Sally's team didn't finish in time for us."

"We spent weeks waiting for mainframe access."

"We spent more time doing data setup and reset than we did testing."

Constraints kill agility. Constraints will keep you up at night. The only thing reassuring about constraints is that just about every enterprise IT development shop has them in spades, so you aren't alone. Your definitions may vary, but there are four root constraints we will explore in this chapter:

- Unavailable Systems and Limited Capacity
- Conflicting Delivery Schedules

- Data Management and Volatility
- Third Party Costs and Control

In-Scope vs. Out-of-Scope

Before we talk about constraints, let's take a minute to understand the nature of **in-scope** vs. **out-of-scope** systems. **In-scope*** *systems are the focus of a development or test activity for a given team.* **Out-of-scope*** *systems are needed for the in-scope systems to operate, but are not the focus of activity.*

When you are building today's highly distributed composite apps, you expect any environment to encompass both in-scope and out-of-scope elements. Every team will have a different composition of what is in or out of scope.

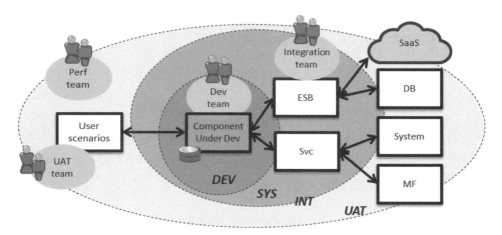

Figure 4-1. In-scope systems increase over time in a software lifecycle. Early component-level development activities have very few systems in-scope, while most other systems are out-of-scope, while each later software project phase of system, integration, and UAT have an ever-increasing amount of in-scope responsibility across multiple systems.

Over a full **Enterprise Release*** lifecycle (Figure 4-1), the status of what is in-scope vs. out-of-scope changes:

- **When we start development**, almost everything is out-of-scope. Only our component, with its own discrete requirements, is in-scope. Almost everything else is either an external dependency or someone else's responsibility and out-of-scope.

- As we move forward to **integration phases**, more systems become in-scope because our need to directly validate successful handoffs between our component and other changed systems. There are still many out-of-scope systems involved as it is rare that every system in the whole business is taking a change for the given release.

- By the time we get to **User Acceptance Testing* (UAT)** project phases, even more systems become in-scope since we must validate that everything is safe for go-live. In the end, we are left with a live application and almost nothing out-of-scope.

Unavailable Systems and Limited Capacity

All large companies that rely on IT must deal with the environmental constraints of unavailable systems, such as mainframes and incomplete components. Teams need to have an appropriate system environment in place in order to develop any new functionality and validate that the application is working correctly.

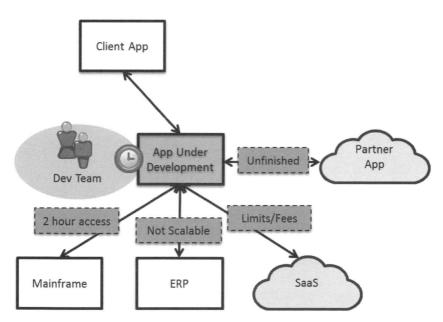

Figure 4-2. Teams building software are inevitably delayed due to limited access windows and unavailability of systems they depend on to finish their own application development processes.

Examples of unavailable systems include the following (Figure 4-2):

- A key mainframe that is used for important customer transactions has only one shared test partition made available to your development team by IT Ops for **only a few hours a week**.

- The test environment for the ERP system is **1/100 of the scale** and performance of production. You cannot sufficiently performance test your application because of the downstream capacity limitations.

- A critical web service that your app will call on is **still under development** by that team—and not expected to be available until just days before your delivery deadline.

- A third party–SaaS-based transaction service provider only allows **5 test transactions per day** on its system before they start charging you for every transaction, not nearly enough to cover your scenarios.

What happens when the preceding situations occur? The project stops, and teams simply wait. There's a reason why you often find active foosball or ping-pong tables in the development areas of a company, but none in customer service.

One SVP of Development for a leading property insurance provider estimates that across the board, his developers and testers were spending as much as **40 percent of their total work hours just waiting**. He put his situation like this: *"I can't do anything until I have everything—and I never have everything!"*

Conflicting Delivery Schedules

While lack of availability is the most commonly identified constraint, it is certainly not the only reason software projects fail to meet expectations. We've discussed how Agile attempts to do away with the typical *Gantt chart** waterfall-type approach by allowing teams to decouple from each other and develop their functionality in faster iterations. This is an excellent plan, but there is still a catch.

Are developers coding in the blind?

Unless the requirement your team is developing for is incredibly simplistic, the app under development is seldom self-contained. The code will eventually interact with components that are owned and managed by other teams—

each of which may be on their own independent develop-test-release timeline. Though you may try to split up the functionality so development teams can decouple and work in parallel with each other, most business applications aren't so easily compartmentalized. There is usually some need to synchronize with the changes of other teams.

Even if early development succeeds at Agile, when we get to the Integration phase and beyond in a composite application project, those teams will crash together—forcing us back into an "AgileFall"-style sequential release process (Figure 4-3). Hurry up and wait.

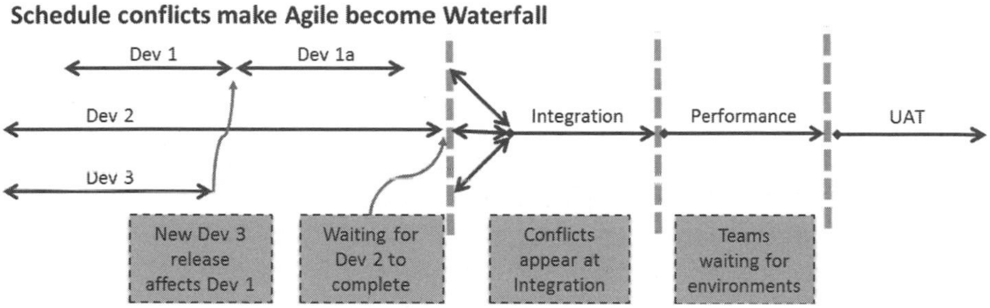

Schedule conflicts make Agile become Waterfall

Figure 4-3. AgileFall process occurs when multiple teams try to iterate in faster scrum cycles, but encounter dependencies on each other's functionality as well as synchronizing needed integration and test lab schedules.

Inefficiencies entrained by the AgileFall process include the following:

- **The knock-on problem:** Teams are hyperaffected by the delivery dates of other teams. One team's delay will have a huge cascading effect.

- **The "every other build" problem:** A broken **build*** in the other team halts your team's progress.

- **The "logjam" problem:** Agile teams experience a "logjam" where no system can be adequately tested for even its application level functionality until all the development teams are ready.

In spite of the interdependency, priority conflicts are endemic in every large enterprise, as different development teams are often answerable to entirely different business goals. Take for example a large retail chain that has one application team building in-store Point-of-Sale (POS) applications for service clerks, and a completely separate dev group responsible for the brand's dotcom web site. Both teams are compensated for delivering on their own agendas, but they also depend on shared access to systems such as inventory and pricing. At these choke points, friction is bound to occur constantly.

Data Management and Volatility

As software becomes more complex and distributed, and handles more customers and transactions over time, it is also generating an exponential increase each year in resulting data. Some systems of record have become so large and unwieldy (petabytes or zettabytes even), that they can barely even be managed. You have dozens of data sources in a wide variety of storage containers. And the data problem is only getting worse. The term **big data*** was coined to describe the massive amount of unstructured data being captured in consumer and transaction activity online. Data is a big, hairy constraint for every enterprise development effort.

Have your teams ever struggled to set up just the right scenarios across multiple systems, only to "burn" them all with a single test cycle? Have you seen issues with regulatory or privacy rules about exactly how customer data is used within development and testing cycles? Or found it difficult to re-create scenarios in test systems for those unique types of edge conditions that happen in production?

In the preceding scenario (Figure 4-4), development teams are attempting to deliver and test a health care web application. Notice how very little of the data is "in-scope" where they can extract it directly—most of the data they

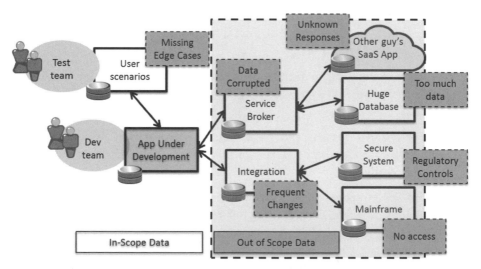

Figure 4-4. Test Data Management problems create huge manual effort and delays due to difficulty setting up complete enough data scenarios from upstream users and out-of-scope downstream systems that are resistant to "copying" into a local database.

need comes from systems that are "out-of-scope" or not under the team's control.

One company has such a severe data problem that they set up a huge "midnight run" requiring 12 other teams to manipulate their own live systems manually, all inserting the test data at the same time in order to accommodate one test run. That's a lot of overtime. One health care QA director told me, "*We spend two hours running a test cycle, then we spend **three full days** resetting data across the systems.*"

The most obvious solution is the conventional practice of **Test Data Management* (TDM)**: extracting a subset of production data directly from all the involved systems into a local TDM database, and then importing that data into the nonproduction systems.

Why the traditional approach to TDM isn't working

- *Fragile data*: Applications change often—requiring frequent, precisely-timed extract, manipulate, and setup activities.

- *"Burned" data*: Live transactions often "burn" a carefully constructed set of test data upon use (your previously zero-balance customer now has a balance!), making the data unusable for that purpose again and requiring either re-import or very difficult, manual undoing of the changes made.

- *Complexity*: Heterogeneous sources—SQL, IMS, VSAM, Flat Files, XML, third-party service interfaces—vary widely, whereas most TDM solutions only deal with a subset of possible **RDBMS*** data sources. Moreover, Big Data brings **nonrelational*** data sources to the mix.

- *Security and regulations*: Strict laws and industry standards govern the protection of private customer data (ID and bank account numbers, medical records, etc.) by development and test teams, as well as accountability standards for how that data is stored and shared.

- *Labor- and cost-intensive*: Many development shops report that 60 percent or more of test cycle time is spent exclusively on manual data configuration and maintenance activities.

- *Difficult-to-reproduce scenarios*: It's hard to isolate and re-create specific input-and-response scenarios. Lack of realism limits the success of functional and performance testing.

We will need to find new ways to free software development from the burden of data management, as this constraint will only become bigger over time.

Third-Party Costs and Control

Not all companies suffer the constraint of data management equally, but third-party costs arise as a "do-or-die" aspect of application development as IT moves toward ever more composite and cloud-based application architectures.

Custom software development and management of applications can be incredibly expensive. Therefore, it makes a lot of sense for the enterprise to offload systems and functionality, whenever possible, to another company that specializes in providing that functionality via a service-based model. This third-party provider then charges the company a fee for any access or remote use of that SaaS offering, cloud service, or managed system resource.

Let's look at a major airline with a critical customer ticketing application that is under constant development (Figure 4-5). They outsource the reservation management aspects of their business to a GDS (Global Distribution Service) like Sabre or Galileo, and the payment management to another company's payment gateway, and so on, paying a fee each time their ticketing app submits a request to these third-party services. These fees are perfectly acceptable in production, where they are justified by the resulting revenue opportunity the airline gets from selling the ticket.

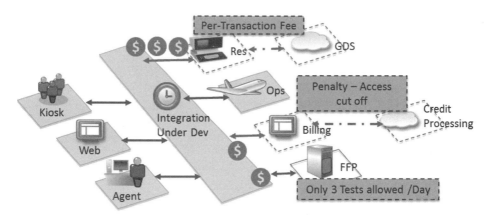

Figure 4-5. Example of third-party costs and control issues at an airline developing their integration server against downstream applications owned by other companies. Each noncustomer transaction or test may incur usage fees or penalties.

But in preproduction, that transaction fee is considered by the business to be a cost of development, not a cost of revenue. Think about the number of unique customer travel scenarios that must be validated, as well as the peak levels of customer traffic the airline must develop and tune their app to perform under.

Four years ago, we heard from an IT manager at an airline who requested a 10,000-user test prior to an important release, and the airline got hit with an unexpected $30,000 bill for service fees—from a single 1-hour performance test! Multiply the fees this airline pays across more than 1,500 developers and testers pinging the systems, and they ended up paying between $7 to $9 million annually just on incurred preproduction costs to third-party services.

This story is by no means unique to airlines. We see third-party fees and preproduction problems on the rise in all IT-intensive industries, from a retailer with excess MIPS charges on the mainframe to a telco getting their development budget eaten up by a provisioning gateway. The owner of a critical health records mainframe charges the insurance payer penalties and even suspends live access when they get hit with too many noncustomer transactions by developers. *Are these other guys just gouging us with these fees?*

Most third-party systems and managed service providers are in the same boat. They exist to support real production business use. They too have highly constrained system resources and assign first priority and capacity to live, revenue-generating customer needs first. They charge fees to your development and test teams because, in fact, they would usually rather not support preproduction environments at all.

One of our delivery/logistics customers is mainly accessed by their customers via their public APIs over the Internet in a SaaS model at no cost to the customer. But their cost to maintain an entirety of their systems for nonemployees to access is a significant cost. Despite being free, it is still one of the most common criticisms of their customers that the test environment provided doesn't offer the capacity, data, or uptime of their production systems.

The net effect of these fees is they create a disincentive to quality for everyone. When **continuous integration*** and validation become associated with unwanted costs, teams are discouraged from thorough testing throughout the software lifecycle, and the end user will feel the impact of poor quality and performance.

Stubs and Mocks Are Not Enough

How can we possibly address all the constraints considered in this chapter? One option would be to spend millions of dollars and undertake a huge configuration effort to try and replicate a copy of the production hardware and software environment with data in a unique physical lab for each team. That's difficult to swallow and solves only the first constraint mentioned—unavailable systems and limited capacity—without relieving any of the others.

Therefore, we see developers turn to **mocking or stubbing*** those downstream systems by coding their own versions of the dependencies with dummy data. These mocking efforts can range from very simple "echo"-type units that always spit back a canned data response to very elaborate collections of stubs in a "responder framework" that are constantly being added and updated to fit the changing needs of dev and test teams. These stubs are usually only effective in development and give no relief to any other phase of the software lifecycle.

Developers should be building new functionality and making sure it works—not building stubs. Stubs and mocks are costly and time-consuming endeavors that are common in most development shops. They don't provide the realism or reusability necessary to carry projects forward with any degree of predictability. Stubs set you up for later integration issues, late defect discovery, and troublesome scalability blind spots.

Often it will be hard to get teams to give up stubbing, as it is "the only way we've known" for most developers. But since huge collections of stubs can become a constraint in and of themselves, we must further discuss how to eliminate them with Service Virtualization.

Business executives often don't appreciate the severity of the preceding software constraints on IT teams—until the constraints create a severe impact that makes the headlines: perhaps a needed product misses its promised date and the competition gets the upper hand; or the quality of the project gets sacrificed for cost or time reasons, resulting in critical failures in front of customers. *It's time for a better way to bring software development into balance with business.*

What Is Service Virtualization?

What if you could have a "flight simulator" for your applications? If it were realistic enough, wouldn't that bring the same level of efficiency and predictability to software delivery that we see in other industries that employ the science of modeling and simulation?

Service Virtualization (or SV) is the practice of capturing and simulating the behavior, data, and performance characteristics of dependent systems, and deploying a Virtual Service that represents the dependent system without any constraints, thus allowing your software to be developed and delivered faster, with lower costs and higher reliability.

In essence, Service Virtualization is the productization of the old practice of "mocking and stubbing" needed components in software development environments, with enough realism and context to push development forward faster. This shifts the ability to test applications to earlier in their development lifecycle, enabling integration and release processes to happen faster, with higher quality and less risk.

The Other Half of Virtualization

It is important to understand the difference between *Service Virtualization* and the well-known technologies on the market today that perform *Server Virtualization**. Both are extremely useful solutions an enterprise can leverage to increase efficiency and reduce IT costs (Figure 5-1).

Server Virtualization is sometimes called Hardware, Desktop, OS or Application Virtualization, and includes a mature class of solutions from

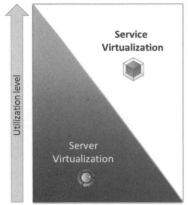

Server Virtualization	Service Virtualization
Increase utilization of under-utilized systems	Reduce utilization of over-utilized systems
Rapid provisioning of Intel images	Provision systems that cannot be imaged via Server Virtualization
Goal is to make a live system available for development & test	Goal is to have behavior of system without live system volatility/costs/time
Assets: Virtual Machines (VMs)	Assets: Virtual Services (VS)

Figure 5-1. This figure compares Server Virtualization with Service Virtualization, contrasting between conventional Server (or Hardware) Virtualization solutions, which address under-utilized systems, and Service Virtualization (SV), which simulates over-utilized systems.

vendors such as VMware, Citrix, Microsoft, IBM, CA, and many others, as well as some open source software tools. In a nutshell, Server Virtualization takes a given system you have access to and copies an image of it—hardware specs, operating system, and current applications it is running, as a *Virtual Machine** (*VM*).

Most Intel-based hardware or server resources on a network are being vastly *under-utilized**. Companies tend to purchase new systems for each project and keep more capacity available than they really need. By making VMs and hosting them in an environment called a *hypervisor**, the IT shop can run multiple VM images on just one server, increasing the utilization of each server and saving money by reducing the number of Intel boxes that must be purchased or housed in a server farm for the in-house computing needs of the company.

Conventional server virtualization is cool and creates a quick reduction in costs. But what about all the things we can't grab and image as a VM? Our enterprise depends on systems that are extremely *over-utilized** and critical for supporting the business. The constraints we mentioned earlier (mainframes, massive data stores, and third-party systems) are too bulky to be imaged as a VM. Moreover, these live environments are usually "locked down" and not available for conventional virtualization. It is in these *over-utilized* environments where Service Virtualization delivers a new level of efficiency and value.

Recall also that even if we can have access to a resource, it may still be heavily constraining. Data volatility, incomplete new features and functions, shared access, and capacity issues are still usually present.

Creation of a Virtual Service

Service Virtualization creates an asset known as a ***Virtual Service* (VS)***, which is a system-generated software object that contains the instructions for a plausible "conversation" between any two systems.

Warning: It is important that there must be real software automation involved in the capture and modeling of the Virtual Service. Otherwise we are still talking about the "stubs" developers would manually code and maintain on their own.

Let's say your team is developing an update to a key application that must make requests of a downstream mainframe and a cloud-based partner service (SaaS). Both of those downstream systems are unavailable for you to use to run your regression and performance tests throughout development. So you replace them with Virtual Services and get to work. Think of the VS as a reliable stand-in for those constrained and costly applications that you don't want to expose to the daily grind and dangers of being set up, used, and reset for testing and integration purposes by developers.

We will cover alternate ways to build Virtual Services, but the fundamental process works this way (Figure 5-2):

1. **Capture:** A "listener" is deployed wherever there is traffic or messages flowing between any two systems. Generally, the listener records data between the current version of the application under development and a downstream system that we seek to simulate.

2. **Model:** Here the Service Virtualization solution takes the captured data and correlates it into a VS, which is a "conversation" of appropriate requests and responses that is plausible enough for use in development and testing. Sophisticated algorithms are employed to do this correctly.

3. **Simulate:** The development team can now use the deployed Virtual Services on-demand as a stand-in for the downstream systems, which will respond to requests with appropriate data just as the real thing would, except with more predictable behaviors and much lower setup/teardown cost.

Remember: We say that a VS is *"simulating"* the constrained system for purposes of development and test, not *"replaying"* it in terms of a step-by-step sequence, as you would a recorded video. Sufficient dynamic logic must be captured and modeled into a VS to allow it to respond with enough intelligence to support the variability of needed usage scenarios. The VS should resemble the live system closely enough to make upstream applications and test users think that they are interacting with the real thing for most needed scenarios.

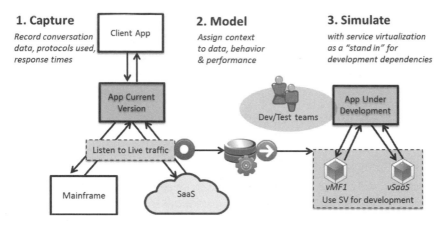

Figure 5-2. This figure shows the basic process for creating a Virtual Service.

Options for Creating and Maintaining Virtual Services

The basic process we have outlined in the preceding three steps is the simplest way to describe how a VS is commonly captured and built out of live transactions. However, when dealing with today's complex IT environments, teams quickly discover that they may not be able to get sufficiently robust models from live transactions alone.

Virtual Services should offer the ability to develop for the future state of the environment as well as the boundary conditions we cannot reproduce simply by watching live traffic. For instance, hooking up the next generation application to a global sales partner will increase orders two orders of magnitude more than we've seen and will give us a number of different sales scenarios.

Options for creating Virtual Services vary depending upon the solution but may include the following (Figure 5-3):

- **Capture from live traffic:** Listen to transactions between systems at any available point where calls and responses occur between any servers, integration layers, or components. These will take the form of protocols such as HTTP, SOAP, JMS, JDBC, **CICS***, and many more.

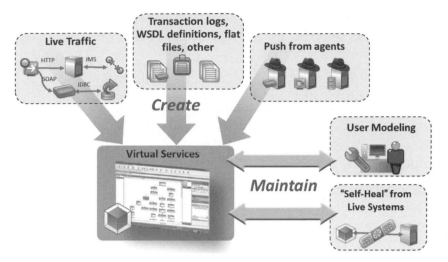

Figure 5-3. How Virtual Services are created and maintained.

- **Interpret from document:** Take requirements or historical data recorded in a file, and parse that into a VS. For a simple starting point, take a WSDL definition or even a spreadsheet of data, and use it to model a first edition of the VS. Or take a day's history of server logs and feed that data into a VS representing that day's observed scenarios.

- **Capture from agents:** Sometimes you may have server-side or internal logic that is not accessible for capture on the wire, but the application can have an "agent" internal to the application or server that pushes relevant events or message data out to be re-created as a VS. This advanced option is not always available, especially in production or heavily secured environments.

- **Create the conversation manually:** Assuming the developers already know the message protocol and payload being used, they can create the VS from scratch.

In addition, teams need to maintain VS models to populate them with additional data and scenarios that the development project must support, as well as account for constant changes. Ideally the SV solution should make this process as intuitive and automated as possible. Options include the following:

- **User modeling:** The owner of the VS manages the "conversation tree" or behavior by using management tools to change logical flows, add or remove request/response data, add or change operations not yet observed in the real world, and adjust the performance responsiveness to meet given scenario requirements.

- **Self-healing:** This capability is especially useful for keeping the VS relevant and reusable in fast-changing application environments. If an "unknown" type of request is made, the VS may pass that request through to the original system, and merge that observed response back into the model under user control.

There are an infinite number of ways to employ these methods to create and manage Virtual Services, some of which we will cover later as best practices in Chapters 8–11 of this book.

What Can You Make into a Virtual Service?

Almost any IT asset that your system can trade information with can be replaced by a VS. Companies have successfully simulated thousands of unique services, data sources, and systems, communicating over hundreds of heterogeneous forms of messaging protocols with a high degree of realism. Don't believe me?

The list in Figure 5-4 is just a start of what you can use Service Virtualization to simulate. Practically any "conversation" between two systems becomes a VS source. You can also generate Virtual Services from system logs or requirements documents if a live transaction stream is not available.

Tip: Hey, won't these guys complain about me virtualizing them? It's important to remember that you aren't copying any actual software code or application runtime assets into a Virtual Service. SV is only making a "live-like" simulation for your own development and testing purposes, based on observed transactions with that system or dependency.

Remember: Most mainframe, system, and service providers welcome Service Virtualization and would rather NOT support nonproduction test partitions for your development teams. Even when high fees are involved, unique preprod instances are a pain for them to maintain too, and they usually represent a net cost to both the consumer and producer.

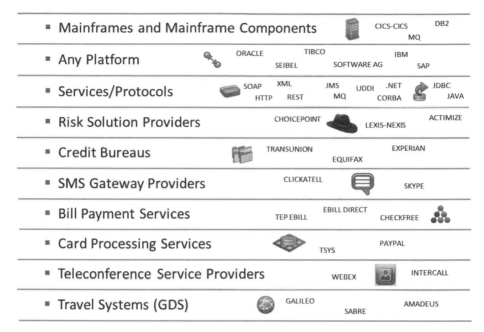

▪ Mainframes and Mainframe Components	CICS-CICS DB2 MQ
▪ Any Platform	ORACLE TIBCO IBM SEIBEL SOFTWARE AG SAP
▪ Services/Protocols	SOAP XML JMS UDDI .NET JDBC HTTP REST MQ CORBA JAVA
▪ Risk Solution Providers	CHOICEPOINT ACTIMIZE LEXIS-NEXIS
▪ Credit Bureaus	TRANSUNION EXPERIAN EQUIFAX
▪ SMS Gateway Providers	CLICKATELL SKYPE
▪ Bill Payment Services	EBILL DIRECT TEP EBILL CHECKFREE
▪ Card Processing Services	TSYS PAYPAL
▪ Teleconference Service Providers	WEBEX INTERCALL
▪ Travel Systems (GDS)	GALILEO AMADEUS SABRE

Figure 5-4. What kinds of things can you simulate with Service Virtualization? This is just a representative list of technologies and service dependencies we've seen turned into Virtual Services by companies. Note that you do not have to "own" or be able to "copy" the whole application; you just need to have a system conduct transactions with it, or use a service requirements definition to start the process.

Virtual Environments Are Better than Real Environments for Dev and Test

Once a VS is created, it can be deployed and run in a *Virtual Service Environment (VSE)**. Think about a VSE as a space for managing a lightweight version of everything you have virtualized from your architecture, whether it is running locally, in the data center, or housed in a private or public cloud.

Most companies approach VSEs as team-shared resources within a software development group (Figure 5-5). Each VSE contains a catalog of several Virtual Services, which at any point in time may be idle or running independently of each other. New Virtual Services can be instantly spun up and ready to respond when invoked appropriately by any upstream system, and then spun down as soon as they are no longer needed.

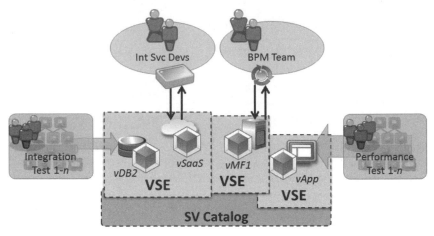

Figure 5-5. Virtual Service Environments are used by multiple teams within an enterprise software development organization. When a team's system under test makes a downstream request, it calls the address of a Virtual Service running in the Virtual Service Environment, which responds with valid data and performance based on the scenario needed.

Wait a minute—is this Virtual Service Environment replacing the live environment all the way up to production?

Actually, we don't recommend that—as tempting as it seems given the efficiencies! Software teams should still perform the "last mile" of User Acceptance testing against live applications. Despite great wind tunnels and flight simulators, we still perform a series of real test flights prior to delivery of a completed aircraft to the public. The value is that we can reach this stage much faster and with higher quality.

Until that last mile of the entire *Software Development Lifecycle** (*SDLC*) process, *using a VSE for development and test is actually much better than using the real thing*. Unlike a physical environment, which is constrained, limited, and highly volatile, a VSE is always ready instantly, 24/7, without conflicts from other teams. It is prestocked with stable, reliable data setups that provide support for all needed scenarios. It can be ratcheted to perform faster or slower.

Best of all, when development teams use a VSE to test often and early, even at component levels, there will be far fewer defects delivered into that last mile, which further reduces the burden on your production-ready environments.

Tech Note: We elaborate on managing VSEs (including local, server, and private and public cloud-based environments) in our chapters on "Best Practices" (Chapters 8-11) and "DevTest Cloud" (Chapter 13).

Capabilities of Service Virtualization Technology

When I first heard of Service Virtualization, I immediately thought, "It's magic; there's no way it's going to work that way." It's difficult to explain as it really doesn't seem like the capabilities are truly possible. So I asked my most skeptical group from development to use it. To justify the approach, we had to prove how many people were being pulled off of value-added projects to build testing and training stubs, which are throwaway efforts anyway.

We abstracted over 20 complex services over the course of the first 5 weeks, and now SV allows us to separate development and engineering for about 75 percent of the lifecycle, and do true end-to-end testing only at the end so we can have much faster time-to-market.

— Sven Gerjets, SVP, DIRECTV

Once the power of virtualizing everything in software development becomes understood, it will create ripples throughout the organization.

Service Virtualization will certainly cause a change in mindset, and raise the bar on everyone for delivering faster releases with higher quality. The most highly valued teams will thrive by learning new skills, such as identifying and replacing external constraints, collaborating with more distributed teams to resolve issues and dependencies, and reducing cycle time by leveraging Virtual Services for parallel development.

What follows are a number of unique capabilities your organization should look for in a Service Virtualization solution.

"Live-Like" Development Environment

Our enterprise software now lives in a heterogeneous, distributed, and highly interdependent world. Just stubbing the next downstream end point with a small set of dummy data responses isn't enough anymore. Development teams require far more realism from their virtual environments, and a much wider variety of upstream and downstream systems must be realistically simulated in their lab environments.

Service Virtualization should be ready and available in between every layer where dependencies exist, to provide an environment that is realistic and "live-like" enough for development and testing to go forward. A big part of that is the requirement for *Stateful** business logic.

Stateless stubs provide only rote responses to requests

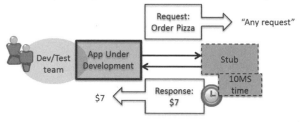

Stateful responses take complex scenarios into account

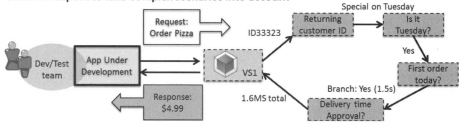

Figure 6-1. Stateless stubs vs. "live-like" stateful Virtual Services. The most obvious distinction between manually coded stubs (shown at top) and realistic Virtual Services (shown at bottom) is usually the live-like Virtual Service response pattern of statefulness, which maintains the context of key dynamic variables such as customer IDs, session IDs, dates, cumulative figures and amounts, and even variable response times where a given scenario may wait for a response.

Most manually built stubs are **stateless***, meaning you can only depend upon getting a rote answer back from them, with little awareness of the current transaction's situation within the business workflow (Figure 6-1). This leads to invalid results—either "false positives" or "false negatives" that can make the effort a waste of time.

When teams work based on real data scenarios and stateful dynamic behaviors captured with SV, their productivity levels are higher, as the resulting environment responds with dynamic data in the appropriate context, and in a more current representation than the collections of stubs that must be manually coded and maintained.

However, note that we said SV should be "live-LIKE," not REAL. Real system data is unwieldy to manage, and the responses are highly volatile and unpredictable. A needed customer scenario that is available in the real system today may be completely invalid and disappear tomorrow, but in our development and test environment, we need that scenario to be there whenever we ask for it. We need the ability to set our environment to represent a specific customer type, in the context of yesterday, or today, or tomorrow, whenever we need it to be. SV offers this ability, which is one reason it is "better than live" for most of the lifecycle.

Expected Capabilities

- Ability to start development despite interface system or downstream system unavailability

- Support for stateful transactions to maintain the context of dynamic elements such as dates/times, session IDs, human input points, and variable wait times as they flow across multiple systems

- Improved code quality due to early access to realistic environments, with increased scenario test coverage and regression testing ability

- Reduced data dependency with fewer access and schedule conflicts due to the status of other applications

Automation Eliminates Manual Stubbing and Maintenance

Before SV, if we were developing a web UI and didn't want to wait around, we would build a stub to generate a couple expected responses from the next layer down, (i.e., the web service). Then the web service developers might stub out their underlying ESB layers, or try to mock up some of the user requests from the web UI, and so on.

> ***Realize that even when we see significant effort in a stub or mock from the development team,*** *the test team cannot use those for themselves because they are ineffective for anything but development's limited set of use cases. This is in fact one of the greatest issues with stubbing: it (on purpose) creates an unrealistic environment for the development team that is only sorted out when the QA group puts the code against the real system behaviors. Only then do we discover how unrealistic the stubs were. Practically every customer we know has this sense of their projects' defect discovery being too late. Leveraging SV both in development and QA will make it happen faster.*

Unfortunately, this is a manual process that is never sufficient to encapsulate the many types of connections and data that exist within enterprise software architectures. Just keeping up with the variability and constant changes of other systems becomes a never-ending process in itself. In addition, the stubbing of those underlying layers may be completely stalled if the UIs or downstream systems aren't yet coded (Figure 6-2).

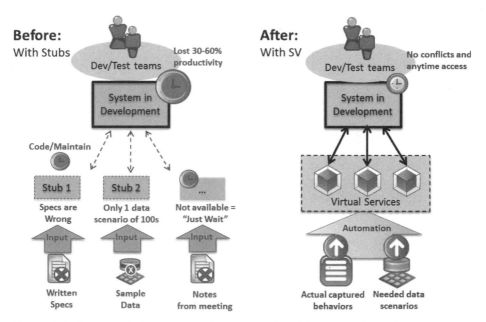

Figure 6-2. Before-and-after automated capture of Virtual Services is shown here. A Service Virtualization solution automatically builds Virtual Services from observed live messages and transactions, system logs, and definition documents, allowing development and test to proceed without wasting time waiting or building and maintaining inadequate stubs.

The critical capability here is the **automation** of VS creation and data maintenance. This automation happens first during the process of listening to messages and capturing the VS from live traffic, or generating the VS from a design document or transaction log. The initial creation should require very little intervention and time on the part of developers. As a rule of thumb, the resulting services should be on average 90–95 percent complete for the scenarios needed by the team—or by definition, the solution is not automated.

Usually letting observation run on a fairly active message stream for a few minutes, or around 1,000 transactions, allows patterns to be recognized and provides plenty of data to populate a VS. Of course, teams may manually model or tweak the VS to add scenarios that couldn't be gathered in the automated capture process—things like very rare edge scenarios and nonfunctional use cases.

Virtual Service, Heal Thyself

Automation isn't just for faster creation. Remember, one of the biggest time wastes for developers is the maintenance of complicated and brittle "stub libraries" in an attempt to keep up with the many changes that occur in a fast-changing environment. Ironically, we must both improve our ability to isolate our teams from each other and yet also increase their ability to deal with the interdependent changes they are all constantly making.

Once a VS exists, the idea of "**self-healing**" comes into play, as we attempt to expand our testing to cover new use cases, or we discover changes and learn new information about the downstream systems that should be reflected in the model of the VS.

Let's say that the VS gets an unknown request that it doesn't have a plausible response for. Rather than just break or return a random default value, the VS can be set to "pass through" and ask a live system for a response, then note that request and response type for possible inclusion in the model of the VS (Figure 6-3).

Auto-healing Virtual Services

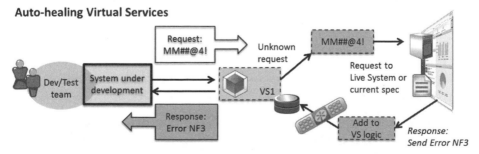

Figure 6-3. Self-healing of Virtual Services allows the data model to be updated from live systems.

Automation allows development teams to achieve realistic virtual lab environments with far less effort, even if the user interface is incomplete, while spending less time working to create and modify outdated stubs.

Expected Capabilities

- Ability to automatically capture, build, and change a simulator quickly with minimal cost and effort that supports most of the needed requirements of the dependent systems

- Natively understands the heterogeneous messaging protocols and format requirements of the requesting and responding technologies with little adaptation or custom extension required

- Self-healing from live systems to keep Virtual Services up-to-date with constantly changing composite applications

- Eliminates manual stubbing, maintenance, and data collection, allowing teams to focus on delivering new functionality

- Leverages the developers' task of creating Virtual Services not just for their use, but as reusable assets that can be used by other teams to respond dynamically throughout later integration and validation phases of the software lifecycle as well.

Enables Parallel Dev and Test

When dev and test teams can work simultaneously using SV, the overall software lifecycle reaches a whole new level of efficacy and efficiency. New solutions can be delivered much faster, at great value to the organization.

In parallel dev and test activities, Virtual Services act as the "go-between" assets between the System Under Development (SUD) and the System Under Test (SUT) in a symbiotic fashion. In Figure 6-4, the timeline on the bottom is a team developing an order management service (OMS), while the team at the top is developing and testing an "e-store" web app that constantly interacts with the OMS.

Here's a rundown of how SV, combined with the parallel development and test process, helps these two teams work faster while staying out of each other's way:

1. A VS (OMS-VS-1) is captured from the current, live OMS system as an initial back end for the e-store's ongoing development.

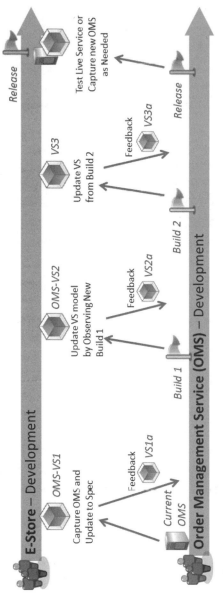

Figure 6-4. Parallel dev and test is shown between two teams using Virtual Services.

2. Then as the e-store's development continues, using the VS for testing as they go, they can communicate back any unexpected or new response requirements as "feedback" to the OMS team as a modified VS (VS-1a).

3. For the OMS team, that VS-1a from the e-store essentially becomes additional customer requirements for their own development and testing.

4. At any time, the e-store can take another VS (OMS-VS-2) by observing the latest actual build of OMS, and use it to update and make changes to the model they are working and testing against.

5. Each parallel development and test cycle continues to accelerate, as each iteration of VS model updates happens with each new build, and feedback happens faster and faster. Both teams can move forward toward release with less dependency, while being better synched up with changes.

The perfect parallel development solution allows teams to execute against the live services at regular intervals when they are available, functionally robust, and data synchronized. And in those cases where teams do not yet have services that support the component correctly, they can switch immediately back to Virtual Services.

This capability to **"flip a switch"** between using a purely virtual downstream system through Virtual Services and the latest version of the live system is an inherent enabler of parallel development. SV means knowing that you always can go back if a new build breaks, or check in changes in a very lightweight fashion if a new data scenario is required.

Is your practice of generating and updating software lab environments keeping in touch with reality? In essence, the parallelism of SV truly enables the quickness we expected of Agile development for complex software environments—by more closely aligning dev and test cycles with business release goals in tight iterative releases.

Expected Capabilities

*   Allows parallel development and collaboration for ever-increasing speed of development and test cycles

*   Enables true "agile" responsiveness of Agile iterations, with continuous integration and builds aligned around test results and business requirements

- Reduces the burden of version control, works with existing development and test management tools to make them more effective

- Increases the rate of issue acceptance and resolution prior to production

- Delivers function points up to 60 percent faster, with higher quality and accuracy to specification due to better alignment among teams

Geek Out: Parallelism demands that SV is a "vendor neutral" substrate for the tools of choice that teams may have in place, so there is less re-training required to reach productivity. SV should provide target environments to work alongside existing application lifecycle solutions such as Test Management (TM), Defect Management/Issue Tracking, and leading Hardware and Test Lab Virtualization products that exist in the environment.

Where to Start with Service Virtualization?

At a recent tradeshow, the CIO of a leading investment bank came up to me after a presentation, talking about the woes of meeting his company's business objectives for new functionality.

He explained to me that every year, before he submits his strategic development plan to the executive management team for review, *he would go through and reduce the number of projects delivered by 50 percent.* And then, going into the last quarter of the year, *he would reduce the expected success rate on those projects by another 50 percent.* There was just no way for him to predict when projects would get done, and how often his teams would have to go back and fix something that went wrong. The horror story of this CIO who must keep rationing executive expectations on new software features downward by 50 percent—much like a trapped miner rationing his water—is not unique to investment banking. Constraints drag down any company with an IT delivery component, and they will only become worse as software becomes more complex.

How can we gain enough velocity to escape from our constraints?

 First of all, Service Virtualization is a TRANSFORMATIONAL approach to delivering business technology that begins with YOU, not someone else. If you take nothing else away from this book, take this.

- **If you are in management**, you must *manage* and *incentivize* SV, or it won't happen.

- **If you are in development,** you must *flip a switch* in your mind to realize that using virtual environments is more productive than using live systems.

We should accept that we are all paddling this leaky software boat together, from developers and testers to IT operations and field teams to our biggest SI partners to the VPs and CXOs who manage the programs and budgets. There is no value to be gained in pointing fingers at one group for the kinds of endemic delays and failures that are happening today. Software constraints hinder every aspect of the enterprise's ability to deliver for customers.

In our engagements, we've found certain organizational decisions will dramatically impact the value a company receives from SV. Without getting into the messy details of an assessment and delivery process, let's take a look at some examples of these.

IT Executives Must Manage and Incentivize SV, or It Won't Happen

Once I ran into a VP of Development at an industry event who started an SV project six months prior. He said to me, *"I made this investment in SV software, and gave it to my developers and IT partners . . . It's great stuff but how come I'm not seeing 30 percent lower costs?"*

To which I replied, *"Did you adjust your actual development budget per feature down by 30 percent? Does anything happen to your developers if they do or don't reduce cycle time by 30 percent?"*

If you are in the position of considering funding an initiative, I can almost guarantee that transformative results WILL NOT happen without a transformation in your own expectations. This may sound harsh, but in other words—**you will not get the results from SV you want if you don't incent and manage to them.**

Who is handling the bulk of your development, testing, and delivery work? If you invested in SV for your teams, as management, it is up to you to require that they consume it in your projects. SV is not a dessert option on their buffet of tools. It is the buffet.

A transition may be painful—so how do I break this to my teams?

How many times has an IT manager been ordered by the EMT and/or Board, seemingly arbitrarily: *"YOU must remove $20 million (or $100 million) from the software development budget."* or *"YOU must lay off 1/3 of the service workforce and use this offshore partner."* or *"YOU must have this software ready within six months or else . . ."* Well, you will also have to exercise some level of prerogative of your own.

It's not like you have to force SV on teams because it is unpleasant or risky—it offers a much faster and less frustrating development experience in so many ways. However, there is a huge amount of inertia to overcome in the existing process, as it is the "devil they know."

We've seen that developers and testers and performance teams may be resistant. If their paycheck cashes either way, they may use a VS to get past one hurdle in a project, then go right back to the way it was—waiting on each other or putting together poor workarounds. This means they are not focusing on the business need at hand.

This may not be fun, and it may make you unpopular for a while. But you must **_incent_** your teams financially and with real goals to make development happen better, faster, and cheaper. And you must consistently **_manage_** their goals publicly, so they share accountability to get it done. Goals like the following:

- *"You will eliminate the 30 percent padding time we used to add at the end of each release cycle for unexpected lag time."*

- *"Any defects released to QA will be reviewed in the group meeting and responsible development teams will need to demonstrate how the component environment was or was not virtualized."*

- *"We are reducing the development budget for the next product release by $1.2 million. If you aren't going to make it, I will need to know why."*

The same also holds true for your business partners and vendors who can benefit from SV enablement. If you hold those contracts, you need to convey your expectations of SV and make partners stick to them.

Let's say you have a supplier partner who charges you for integrating their order systems to your purchasing service. If they can now leverage your VS instead of writing their own stubs, you should tell them, *"I know we've just reduced your development cost—so if this doesn't pass on a cost reduction to my company, let's review the terms!"*

Identify Stakeholders (The SV War Council)

So you have located the problems. Now how will you overcome the resistance to change that is inevitable in any extended enterprise?

Even if one individual owns ultimate responsibility for an implementation, we have found that the most successful adoptions of SV happen when ownership is shared among a small group of leaders grounded in different disciplines. We will call this the "SV War Council," but you can call it a Task Force, Tiger Team, Drum Circle . . . whatever works in your culture. The promise of faster innovation, fewer customer problems, and lower costs can benefit everyone, so look for champions who understand these benefits. This team will open doors and provide workarounds, so the project can move forward smoothly.

While the council responsible for carrying out the SV strategy may vary depending on the politics and organizational structure of your company, it works best when it spans several competencies:

- **Line-of-Business Executive:** Someone responsible for delivering current customer-facing projects that depend on software.

- **IT Operations/Environments:** Someone responsible for provisioning or managing software development environments.

- **SVP/Development Owner:** Someone who owns overall software development/delivery functions and who clearly understands the scope of the constraints.

- **Trusted Architect:** This is one of the "masterminds" in the company who tends to know the current state and future plans for the company's software road map and integration infrastructure.

- **QA and/or Performance Team Lead:** One or two leads who are experiencing the day-to-day constraints of lack of capacity, unavailable systems, and compressed timelines.

- **Service Partner Lead:** If applicable, the smartest lead consultants from your strategic SI partners who are helping to carry development or testing projects forward should also be eager to participate and provide perspective. (And if your partner discourages SV efficiencies because it may reduce some billable work hours, you might call that a bad sign . . .)

Secure an executive sponsor responsible for business *P&L**, not just the IT guys. While successful SV initiatives offer huge efficiency benefits to the IT organization, they usually start with executive sponsorship and an alignment to real, customer-facing business objectives (read: Revenue). Time-to-market benefits usually lead the pack for what motivates this executive sponsor—because if a business can depend on delivering a critical new product or service to customers 30–50 percent faster, without fail the revenue and cost benefits will certainly follow, as will a lasting competitive advantage.

Who Should Use Service Virtualization First?

Do we start our journey with the cliché of "low-hanging fruit?" Not this time.

Ever try out a new stain remover? The instructions will say to "test on the material in a less noticeable area" first. Well, we think the opposite should apply to your earliest SV efforts.

Advice: Pick a hairy problem first. Go find the biggest, most stubborn goat of a software problem that exists in your environment. You know, the one everyone's complaining about that makes delivery run late and over budget. Locate a key software-enabled initiative with many moving parts, including big mainframe availability and data conflicts that are eating untold hours and dollars. Tell them you can use SV to decouple those complex constraints in days or weeks of modeling, not months or years of coding. Nobody will believe this is possible.

Why start with a hairy problem? This group should be ready and willing to try something new. When the constraints are already well known, failure is certain if something doesn't change. The potential improvements of eliminating the constraints will be massive. Yes, you could pick something easy, but would that make believers out of the organization?

Involve experienced resources for starters.

Since the challenges it must solve are complex, SV initiatives happen best when accompanied by seasoned people who can lead the rollout strategy. By bringing experienced resources to bear, initial rollouts lead to early successes, and participants in the process will become experts who can teach other teams. Over time, the practice will become a core competency of the organization.

One typical place to start is with **whoever owns development and/or performance environments**. These teams are usually over-utilized themselves—trying to provision, configure, and maintain an ever-increasing sprawl of servers, images, and lab capacity for multiple projects. Replacing much of that activity with SV lifts a huge burden, while positively impacting the productivity of many others who depend on these environments to do their job.

Another good approach we've seen is when the rollout team recruits **developers who are already manually coding and maintaining stubs and mocks**. These tireless workers already understand the nature of having to code around missing components and constrained mainframes by "faking out" those systems. There may be a little resistance to letting go of all of that hard work, but it wasn't wasted effort. Building stubs made these teams understand the location and difficulty of constraints.

Chances are that coding and maintaining these "responder frameworks" was the least satisfying part of the developers' jobs, and quite thankless. The assets produced early in development were brittle and inadequate for supporting later integration and testing cycles. By giving them a way to automate that process with SV, they can carry forward a new set of reusable Virtual Services, and instead focus on building tighter integrations and killer new functionality that will make them look like heroes.

There are other scenarios for initial SV users besides these. Generally the ideal first adopters will be groups with a better than average technical grasp of your architecture, and first-hand experience with the constraints that plague software development and delivery.

Set Real Value Goals for Releases

Set value goals for the first SV project up front. While it is tempting for a team to kick off the install ASAP and start virtualizing some annoying constraints, don't skimp on the value. The rest of the organization is watching and will often meter their expectations of SV based on the success of that first project. Setting a goal and measuring the value from the beginning enables your organization to support future projects with confidence.

How does my company expect to create value from Service Virtualization?

Every company has different priorities for value. These priorities are usually set at the executive or business operations level, then translated into goals that the IT and software development functions can use in their own planning.

Value goals may be forward-looking—for instance, a company in a growth market may state "an obsession with innovation" and value the agile delivery of advanced new features above all else. Other companies will care more about process metrics like maximizing efficiency and reducing defects. Or, a company may only look at hard-dollar benefits and cost savings.

There is an old maxim in software development of "faster, better, or cheaper: you can't get all three." While that used to hold true, SV has the power to change this equation. So for purposes of this book, we'll just call the three value goals "Faster, Better, Cheaper" (Table 7-1).

Table 7-1. Sample Value Goals for a Service Virtualization Initiative. These are typically discrete numbers based on the strategic objectives of the company for the IT/software delivery function.

Faster	Better	Cheaper
Decrease software cycle times from 6 months to 3 months	Reduce defects delivered to QA and production by 50%	Lower labor and overtime costs for testing and break-fix by 30%
Increase the number of function points delivered per release by 20% per year	Bring systems into compliance with new privacy and data regulations by this year	Avoid planned $20M capital outlay for new software integration and performance labs
Successfully get to market with a critical new service by August ahead of competition	Increase customer satisfaction survey results to average 4.0 and reduce complaints by 25%	Eliminate third-party fees and capacity charges in nonrevenue systems by $7.5M/year or 90%

These are just some example value goals we've seen stated before adoption in the field. Most companies follow the limitation that they can't get all three—and only pick goals for one benefit such as cost reduction over the others. With SV, those boundaries on software development will finally become obsolete.

Remember: *If the only justification for investing in SV is to "get a better TOOL" for a given task, the resulting value will be limited by definition.* To the company at large, SV will just be a patch that helped complete the next step in a project, and therefore progress with SV becomes dormant when the project ends. The real value of SV is only realized when a genuine transformation is expected, one that changes the way applications are developed and tested, now and in the future.

Avoid Inappropriate Technologies

As of the publish date of this book, SV is still an emerging solution space in the software development industry—so unfortunately you won't find objective views from the usual sources in the press and analyst community on what SV vendors have to offer today. In addition, you will find software in the market that claims to be SV, when it is actually outside of SV as defined by your humble authors (who invented, coined the term, and patented the first SV technology).

We've already covered how *SV is the concept of virtualization, only applied to* <u>*software*</u> *instead of* <u>*hardware*</u>. Server virtualization solutions such as VMware require that you have access and ability to image a resource from things like Intel boxes, hardware, and desktop software. Here are some other applications that are **not** representative of a SV solution:

SV does not replace your ALM software

Most software shops own a set of tools for **Application Lifecycle Management (or ALM).** This broad and mature technology space covers the scheduling, organization, and workflow tasks of software development—from requirements and test management to source code control to issue tracking and release management to other similar project tasks that teams need to collaborate on. Whether your firm standardizes on a big vendor like HP or IBM or leverages a combination of boutique software and open source, these tools are very useful for managing the process, but not the environment. ALM benefits greatly from SV, which contributes the environments and VS assets to the process, in order to shift that project left for earlier testing and delivery. Since different teams select different ALM tools, your SV environments should work with any ALM, test, or requirements tool of choice.

More than a simplistic "record-playback" tool

Another set of solutions on the market automates a very specific task of recording a stream of message requests and responses, then in effect "playing the session back" in the same order as it was observed. This is the back-end equivalent of the old way UI testing tools would record "click stream" activity and make that into a procedural sequence that followed the user's mouse and keystrokes around the screen. It may be useful for some tasks such as replaying the exact responses of a given scenario, but it doesn't represent the dynamic variability of the application environment needed.

Will not require a specific vendor integration or business application platform

Composite enterprise applications are by nature becoming more distributed and heterogeneous every day. Therefore, a SV platform should take this into account and not require you to "rip and replace" existing integration and business applications with the other systems of a specific vendor in order to realize the benefits of robust simulation. If you can only successfully virtualize one stovepipe of proprietary technology, your teams will still be constrained by any systems falling outside of that vendor's standards.

Intermission

Go ahead and take a break. You now know what Service Virtualization technology is, and what it can do to accelerate the software development lifecycle. You've earned it.

MEDITATION EXERCISE:

Based on what you've learned so far, meditate for a while on other parallels of using simulation to solve real-world problems in other industries. Service Virtualization is like . . .

. . . a wind tunnel used in car design, as you can't test aerodynamics from inside the car. SV is a wind tunnel for your apps where you can control the environment around it . . .

. . . a stuntman or stand-in on the movie set, to replace expensive actors for dangerous stunts or nonproduction scenes when you don't need a close-up, at lower risk and cost . . .

. . . a flight simulator for planning aircraft design and training pilots to fly in noncritical simulated settings . . .

. . . the holodeck from Star Trek, only for app dev . . .

. . . a fake Wild West town, where your app can "shoot it out" with dependencies, but the "buildings" and "mountains" are all cheap set pieces . . .

. . . a test harness from the world of electronics design . . .

. . . arranging and planning your design layouts with thumbnail images instead of full-size ones . . .

. . . the dreams of software . . .

Next, let's cover the Four Best Practices of Service Virtualization. These are the most successful adoption trends we've noticed at some of the largest enterprises, facing the biggest challenges. In the "New Virtual" science of software development, a strong methodology backed by experienced teams that continually learn and adapt is the key to realizing lasting customer success.

Best Practice 1: Deliver Faster

I once worked with a contractor who did a great job on a couple interface design projects, but unfortunately, both took him twice as long as he estimated. Though he gave me a discount, I still had to pick up much of the work along the way, and his excuse was always "I just got too busy." Of course, about six months later, he wasn't busy at all—and asked me if I had any more work for him. "Sure, next time I have a project that doesn't have a deadline, I'll call you . . ."

With software, we always want to **deliver faster**. In composite application environments, Waterfall development approaches slow down results because of the constraints of unavailable or unready systems throughout the software development lifecycle. By the time software is integrated, fitted with an interface, and reaches QA, the defects that surface are much more difficult and costly to fix. The component-level code development and integration work is already baked into the product.

To answer this, development teams naturally tried Agile development to attempt to produce a more frequent rhythm of smaller releases with tighter scope. The Agile approach of rapid unit-test-first development, standups, and scrums is indeed a faster way for developers to work—if they were building stand-alone applications without constraints.

For most of today's composite applications, when multiple teams' Agile releases hit the integration, performance, and user acceptance phases, they stack up and wait to be synchronized for testing. The developers may think they are "done and onto the next" bit of coding, when they are often still delivering unready components over the wall into QA.

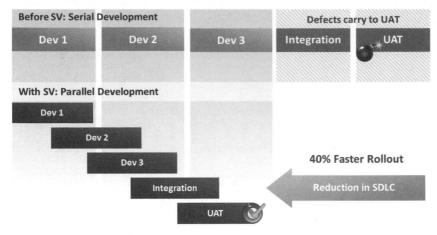

Figure 8-1. Faster Delivery with "shift-left" means testing is enabled far earlier in the SDLC by the use of Service Virtualization, as each team can validate and tune their own development in parallel at a component level, while also reducing the number of defects that must be fixed later in QA or UAT, resulting in overall faster releases.

By eliminating the constraints common in typical software development approaches, much of the SDLC becomes parallel again, even with multiple teams working in the most complex distributed environments. Much of the testing at a component and integration level should "**shift-left**," or be moved earlier in the SDLC (Figure 8-1). To shift-left, Service Virtualization is applied so each component is tested individually in the context of its real environment, instead of waiting for issues to surface later during assembly when they are costliest to remediate.

Shift-Left truly enables the Agile goal of TDD (Test-Driven Development), as developers can prove their software with realistic testing and fix issues before checking in code, or moving onto the next task and declaring a component "ready for integration." Regression and performance testing happens earlier with far more complete coverage, so more defects and potential conflicts are caught before integration or user acceptance testing activities.

Reducing Wait Time through Virtual Privacy

We've discussed how much time developers spend waiting on each other. Most enterprise developers we talk to admit spending at least a third of

©iStockphoto.com/Nicole S. Young

their time waiting on downstream system and data dependencies, even when using Agile development approaches.

With SV, developers can truly be autonomous, leveraging their own private environments for developing code. We call this aspect of Shift-Left *"Virtual Privacy"* because just like putting on headphones or closing the office door and holding phone calls, the isolation it grants is ideal for allowing developers to concentrate on the task of coding toward business goals with fewer distractions.

Imagine this private virtual environment where developers:

- Get an on-demand lab that contains very current, known aspects of the "as is" or "to be" test harness of the target application environment they will deliver their code into

- No longer need to call IT Operations to procure and provision new servers and software, or beg and borrow capacity and time from another team

- Never queue up for shared environments during development

- Never maintain their own VM images of environments they only need as a dependency

- Never wait on the bench for other developers to finish their new services—they can even start work based on a contract or definition of how the service-to-be will function when complete

- Never again write and maintain libraries of stubs and mocks, which are usually too simplistic and brittle for most tasks anyway

- Perform early and complete validation and regression testing of their code for fewer defects per cycle

Since Virtual Services are generally far more lightweight than their real-world counterparts, it is easy to store and retrieve them at will with far less system overhead. Some developers even keep a small "personal cloud" as a VSE on their laptop, which is perfectly suitable for supporting most component development tasks.

Certainly, when you implement SV environments into your project plans, you can expect the practice to start shifting toward parallel development, as well as individual developer productivity and quality (and job satisfaction, most likely).

Kill Stubs Now, or Pay Later

After years of manually building unit tests and mocking frameworks alongside their code, some developers will be hesitant to change—and will want to continue mocking up quick stubs. But unless they are working on very simplistic apps, there is so much detail needed by the consuming application that **calling it "something I can mock up quickly" means they don't understand the true nature of the problem.**

Replacing component-level stubs isn't just a nice-to-have feature for quality and time savings. For complex applications, it is mandatory that we replace stubs in order to reliably deliver on business requirements.

When developers make stubs early in development, they quickly code them for a simplistic or "happy path" view of the responses in the target environment. The best they can do with this artifact is make a "round trip" from their component software to the stub to prove connectivity to that stub. Once the code checks out against the stub, the developers usually move on to the next task.

Unfortunately when carried forward into integration, UAT, and release phases, that early developer use of stubs invariably produces unintended consequences. The problems that may appear later in the SDLC aren't just quality issues— they are often missed requirements. The cost to the business of correcting a defect or missed requirement in QA or deployment is astronomical—1,000 times or much more, in comparison to fixing that issue during early development (Figure 8-2).

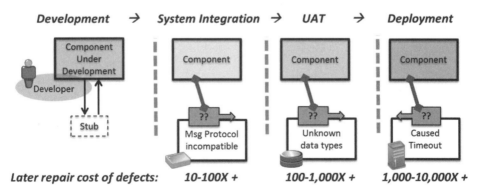

Figure 8-2. The high cost of developing with stubs. When developers code against very simplistic manually built stubs, they get little context into the real environment and then move on to other projects once that code is thrown over the wall. Repair and remediation costs later in the software lifecycle increase exponentially as a result.

Let me explain: *If every customer response for a stub has the exact same profile and the exact same address, account balance, etc. all with hard coded values and* *dates, then that stub only proves ONE needed scenario. But what about customers with high account balances? What about old invoices? What about transactions that occurred yesterday—and will they work the same tomorrow when that date becomes two days ago?*

The problem with a stub is that it can never realistically be coded dynamically enough to support the increasingly complex variety of scenarios needed for a real-world application. Now is the time to stop making assumptions about how developed components will work once they are integrated. Regain that wasted time spent coding stubs, and have developers Shift-Left to build in quality from the start using SV instead.

Sprint: Putting Shift-Left in Practice

> We are trying to avoid what we call "system test gridlock." App A waits on App B, they wait on App C, and everybody delays real-system testing. We looked at adopting Service Virtualization as a way to take all of those excuses out of the lifecycle for the development teams we depend on. So we started with an in-store app as our pilot and built 80 Virtual Services in the first two-week project, which enabled us to do system testing for that app in a stand-alone way we could never do before.
>
> Now a year later, we have more than 300 Virtual Services built. The primary benefit of SV was our ability to cut down the release cycle time and improve the quality of the code much earlier in the lifecycle. In very complex integration environments you need this ability.
>
> We had an incredibly important external integration project coming up. With SV, we were able to promote a Virtual Service as a specification of how we would expose APIs to our partner. We had that Virtual Service built and running within 24 hours of getting those design requirements, and our partners were thrilled with that result. SV has enabled us to "Shift-Left" and get our most important products to market faster.
>
> — Jamie Williams, IT Director, Sprint-Nextel

Let's take a slightly more detailed look at Sprint. With more than 300 complex enterprise services currently under management or development behind the scenes of its customer-facing apps, the development teams were facing serious integration and timeline issues in their test environments. The goal was to shave time off testing and release cycles so that the projects would come in on time for the launch of critical new customer features.

Sprint was introducing new capabilities to their retail store management system, which relies on extensive calls into back-end systems to get customer data and provision new handsets. Typically, any meaningful system testing on

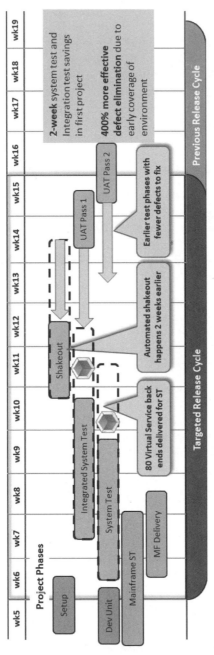

Figure 8-3. A Shift-Left pilot project with Service Virtualization at Sprint. Project teams are shown in horizontal "swimlanes" as they apply Virtual Services to reduce timelines and increase test coverage levels. (Some proprietary project phase names have been removed from these captured project results.)

code changes in this application was blocked until the shakeout of many back-end systems and middleware was completed in the end-to-end (ETE) test environment.

By virtualizing the services that the retail store application depended on, meaningful system testing was able to occur much earlier in the lifecycle than ever before (Figure 8-3). The first pilot project's System Test phase was completed two weeks earlier than before and covered more scope. The coverage and quality results of system testing during the pilot were a whole lot better as well. Testing during the pilot with Virtual Services allowed system test teams to find a lot more defects and ultimately increase defect effectiveness rates for system testing by 400 percent from previous releases! In fact, defects became so scarce that there were zero significant integration defects found in a later integration testing phase. This was a result that was unheard of before the use of Virtual Services.

Pleased with their pilot project results, Sprint embarked on an aggressive journey to roll out Virtual Services for all key middleware transactions, engaging development teams across the company to insulate their applications from back-end dependencies during system testing and shift more defect discovery to the left into development and system test phases of the lifecycle, just as had been seen with the pilot. The IT middleware organization at Sprint started a Service Virtualization *Center of Excellence (CoE)**, rolling out more than 300 Virtual Services in a catalog available to dev and system test teams throughout the company. Sprint now enjoys decreased costs for testing and defect resolution, along with faster cycle times for project testing and deployment.

Best Practice 2: Reduce Your Infrastructure Footprint

Solving the problem of available IT infrastructure for software development doesn't seem like the sexiest thing Service Virtualization can do outside its ties to "Green IT" initiatives for reducing energy consumption. However, the potential business value goes way beyond environmental impact, and the ROI it can generate sure is sexy once it is understood by management.

Every large company continuously accumulates additional infrastructure to support ongoing business and new service offerings. This includes buying more web servers and app servers, additional mainframe partitions, increased network capacity, more software licenses, exponentially larger databases, and additional transaction space on third-party and shared resources.

When conventional Server Virtualization emerged on the scene starting around the year 2000, businesses jumped on it with haste, and that consolidation created an immediate reduction in *capital expense (CapEx)** by reducing hardware and server room costs. However, if we follow *Moore's law**, we also know that these commodities will also become faster, more compact, more efficient, and cheaper every month as technology advances.

So while the use of VMs and hypervisors hastened the reduction of "under-utilized" system resource costs and saved some power in the server room, it couldn't touch the even costlier and faster growing infrastructure availability problems of "over-utilized" systems needed to support distributed enterprise applications.

Finding Over-Utilized Resources

Businesses that identify infrastructure availability as a growing problem are basically complaining about over-utilized system constraints in their software environments. These over-utilized resources cannot be easily replicated, controlled, or accessed by development teams and partners when needed. This results in endemic project delays and failures.

These constraints are very sore spots and should be easy to identify—as you will find teams waiting around for access or data setups to happen. As a general rule, we recommend prioritizing SV rollout where the most conflict and wait time is occurring first by conducting a formal or informal survey of development and product managers. Here are some things to look for:

- Core business applications that are handling critical daily transactions for customers; therefore, they "lock out" development teams due to necessity.

- Enterprise back-end systems (SAP, Oracle apps, managed services, and mainframes) with too few test instances to support the number of distributed development and test teams that need them.

- External SaaS applications or data services that charge per-use fees for preproduction traffic, have availability problems, or impose harsh "caps" and shut off access after a few noncustomer requests.

- IT Operations and environment groups that are overwhelmed with software lab provisioning requests from multiple teams, often with little or no budget to improve their situation.

- Performance labs that are seemingly stocked with technology, but suspiciously sitting idle most of the time due to access issues outside the performance lab.

- Regulation or **IT governance*** policies that prevent distributed teams, SI partners, and offshore resources from accessing the systems and data they need to work with to move forward.

Make a report card of all the preceding choke points you discover in your initial survey, and set a value to solving each of them in your environment. The value of eliminating a constraint would include the following:

- Number of teams or resources waiting on access to the infrastructure constraint and potential wasted hours of labor.

- Criticality or lost revenue of projects the constraint is delaying or derailing.

- Cost of replicating another copy of the constraint or buying more test regions and partitions.

- Amount of time spent manually configuring the resource, including importing and cleaning up datasets for different teams' testing activities.

- Reduced impact of development activities and changes on infrastructure that handles live customer transactions.

The preceding list does not need to be a mathematical calculation. Simply rate the constraints for starters on an estimated 1–5 scale of severity. One piece of infrastructure likely to make your most wanted list for optimization will be the mainframe.

Mainframe Development Needs Virtualization Too

Yeah, this part is boring. It's about old mainframe technology; there's really not much development happening in there. It's stodgy, monolithic stuff . . .

 A confession: At this point in the book, I have to admit, like many of my colleagues in the distributed development world, that I have improperly characterized the mainframe for much of my professional life. We spend so much time obsessed with building new features, on richly functional composite applications, new integration buses, SaaS, cloud, and so on. We even lumped the mainframe into the "Legacy Apps and Back Ends" box in our old diagrams.

Well, we now realize nothing could be farther from the truth. Many enterprise IT leads we talk to say they *still spend as much as 50–60 percent of their development and change integration time within mainframe environments*. In fact, when you take a closer look at most mainframes you find they are not monolithic at all. Mainframes encompass whole landscapes of service-oriented apps in and of themselves.

For most enterprises, **business rides on the mainframe**. In these groups, you have all the same constraints in the service-oriented world—different teams

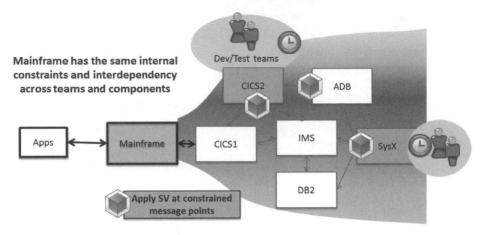

Figure 9-1. Mainframe internal architectures also contain components that can be managed by separate teams and create dependencies that inhibit the changes developers need to make to meet business requirements.

maintaining business logic for interconnected components across different CICS regions; data sources like DB2, ADABAS, IMS services; and so on (Figure 9-1). Mainframe development teams often find themselves constrained for access, waiting for critical data scenarios to be set up in other mainframe regions, and in conflict over resources.

IT Operations teams don't want to rock the boat for real customers by allowing developers and testers to play "under the hood," yet new test region environments are extremely difficult and expensive to produce. SV should be practiced in a similar fashion within the mainframe, capturing and modeling dependencies between components. For instance, simulating the other half of CICS-CICS transactions or gathering scenarios from an IMS region as it makes calls to the data layer.

In short, don't leave efficiencies on the table inside the mainframe. We must ensure that we get under the hood and liberate mainframe development of constraints with SV in addition to the upstream application layers.

Avoiding Big IT Outlays

Enterprises used to have only one alternative for addressing constrained infrastructure, besides simply waiting:

Write a huge check.

Without realistic infrastructure, our applications won't successfully get to market—but the cost of building more of these complex environments through conventional means is becoming so high that it almost seems like a joke when you hear folks tell you what it takes. We know that VPs of development and IT directors are delivering unwelcome purchase requests like these to executives all over the world when asked, "What do you need to do this right?"

Try building an environment that is even just 25 percent of the size of production. That's configuring every server and licensing every component—a massive effort and cost just to get a version that will still never be an adequate simulation of production.

It's not like companies aspire to attain a big infrastructure—that's just what happens when a company gets big. Take for instance a company like PayPal when it was in startup mode in 1998. A small development team probably built the first prototype of their app in two to three months. But fast forward to PayPal today as part of a huge enterprise inside eBay, and—it functions more like a bank now. There are more hooks to other systems and baggage to contend with for each successive release they add, more customers relying on promised support, bigger databases and more services and systems they must talk to, each of which may be owned and managed by different groups.

The problem with infrastructure costs for development, test, and partner labs (Figure 9-2) is that they create a very big hit to *CapEx*—in the form of big purchases and big-bang implementation projects. But that's not all—each new infrastructure buy creates a very large and growing **operational expense (OpEx)*** for maintaining and upgrading the lab environment constantly in order to keep up with configuration changes, increased data, etc. The more environment infrastructure you buy, the more that infrastructure becomes a job in and of itself, with its own dedicated maintenance and support team.

*A leading firm we know wanted to ensure flawless partner integration and performance, so management demanded that IT build a certification environment representing **100 percent of production**. The IT department came back with an estimate of **$60 million for starters**, plus at least **$15 million/year** maintenance to try to keep it current! That was just not going to happen!*

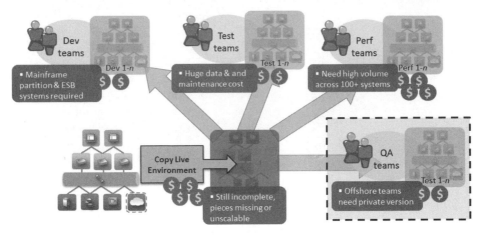

Figure 9-2. Massive infrastructure costs occur when live and preproduction systems are replicated for use by development, performance, and test/QA organizations within and outside the company. Changes happen so fast it is nearly impossible to keep up in today's multitier environments.

Many companies don't count "cost avoidance" as hard value results. But that $60 million outlay estimate wasn't ridiculous given the complexity at hand. Whether the firm would have bitten the bullet or not, it was clear they couldn't survive for long without a more complete environment. Using SV (Figure 9-3), they were able to replace most of that expected development infrastructure outlay with virtual models and virtual data management within two quarterly release cycles, at a fraction of the cost.

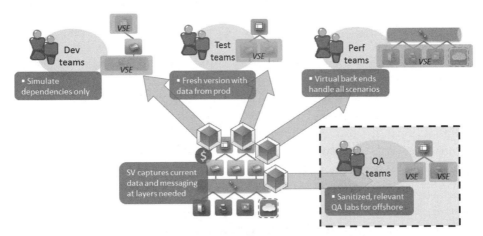

Figure 9-3. Infrastructure cost savings after Service Virtualization are significant, as the groups only request "just what they need" from a simulation of the live app environment, which runs with very low overhead. Most of the configuration, data maintenance, and change updates of the Virtual Services are automated, saving both CapEx and OpEx.

Customer Example: Dodging a Wave

I was visiting the architecture team of one of the world's largest banks when I heard a stunning statistic. This gentleman related to me that the hardware asset management system claims **there are more servers deployed in the bank than there are employees in the bank.**

He then explained how his firm's typical project-based budgeting process created the perfect fertile ground for growing huge server farms. Every project team would justify the expense of its own development, testing, preproduction, and production environment expenditures. Almost every one of the 1,000+ applications currently in use at the bank still has at least four environments sitting behind it, even if the maintenance or changes on some of those applications now only happen annually!

One solution was to attempt a massive consolidation process. It would be a huge endeavor to centralize and rationalize all those development and test servers, image them as VMs, and then have the responsibility for that process roll up to the CIO. The cost would practically be prohibitive and because it would be replicating only the systems that could be Server (not Service) virtualized, there would still be many dependencies they could not replicate.

This bank is now getting tremendous value from Virtual Service technology. Hundreds of pre-production labs fold into a vastly simpler to manage infrastructure, with software-based provisioning on an on-demand basis for any of the required environments. Projects not currently under change no longer consume power, generate heat, or consume floor space—or cost millions of dollars and require dedicated staff allocations to support and maintain.

Best Practice 3: Transform Performance and Scale

In most enterprises, the Performance group's needs are prioritized highly in terms of IT budget and hiring expert staff because the stakes are very high. Performance teams are usually the last line of defense against delivering a losing game in the marketplace.

You need to get a feeling for how critical performance is. The customers we are talking about are not just uploading the latest funny picture to a social media site—they are running applications that handle critical business. Without high *performance*, your systems cannot sustain over time and will not be able to *scale* to meet increasing customer demands and requirements.

Virtualizing Performance Environments: Are You Waiting to Fail?

Performance will make or break an application. We need to do everything in our power to ensure that our software can scale and sustain high performance levels over time, even in an environment of constant change and volatile usage levels.

Yet almost everyone, *even many very smart people in the software community*, still think of performance testing as an "after-the-fact" activity. We run a finished or near-finished application under a certain amount of load [transaction per second (TPS) or a number of "virtual users"] and record the app's response times for each request.

The idea is to confirm the speed of our application, whether that is to meet a contractual **Service Level Agreement (SLA)*** or simply a customer satisfaction goal:

- "We've determined that users leave our site 25 percent more frequently when the web site's response time is greater than 3.0 seconds, so ensure it never exceeds 2.0 seconds."

- "Our competitor's Customer Rate Quote time is 2.5 seconds. Ours needs to be faster."

- "If maximum response time of the app under test is less than 500ms with 1,000 TPS load for 1 hour, it passes our clients' SLA agreement."

If our performance tests and monitors confirm we are consistently meeting our goals, that's great. *But what if performance is failing?*

Since conventional performance testing happens from an end-user interface perspective, it can only tell us that something is wrong somewhere—not where the problem is in the composite application or how we can solve it. There is only so much you can do to "tune" a web page, perhaps by reducing image sizes or changing how the HTML of a page is loaded. Most of the business logic is played out in machine-to-machine transactions. *The common practice of validating and tuning the performance of your applications just prior to production is when you have the least ability to actually make any improvement in performance.*

Developers try to be Agile and do more testing earlier, which catches some structural code errors and bugs in functional and unit tests. But when a developer checks in some code that will become a performance defect, it is often impossible to detect until several months later, when it rears its ugly head under real-world integration pressures (Figure 10-1).

Furthermore, the performance lab will often sit idle, waiting on the bench for everyone else to finish their software releases and integrate. This end game only perpetuates the problem of having to hurry performance testing at the end of several serial development cycles.

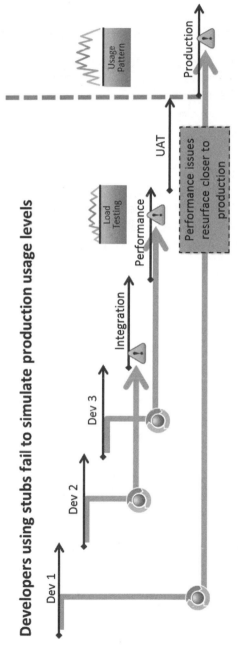

Figure 10-1. Performance defects escape Development with stubs. When developers only "unit test" and write mock stubs in early stages, they will be unaware when they are checking in poor-performing code to the project. These defects can escape to later stages or even cause performance issues in production, where they are the costliest to fix.

Service Virtualization offers a proactive solution to this dilemma, and should drastically change your perspective on what it means to do performance testing for today's composite applications.

Component-Level Performance Budgeting

If a performance defect is going to occur, we need to isolate it and find it much earlier in component-level testing. That seems impossible, as many performance lags are related to interactions between live systems—and won't surface until integration or deployment. Let's use SV to decouple these systems, while still proactively looking at their performance when they come together.

A technique we call *performance budgeting* enables teams to practice performance engineering in a manner congruent with the incredibly high amount of distributed components and teams making changes to today's composite applications. To tune the aggregate performance of an application, fractional response times must be "budgeted" out to each component.

We also call this concept *Service Level decomposition*. Expected Service Levels must be broken down into smaller units, then verified and enforced at the component level.

As shown in the example in Figure 10-2 from a leading telco customer, performance testing a near-finished solution falls short. In the top line, we see the completed Solution (made up of Verify, Lookup and Quote steps) coming back with a poor response time of 4.0 seconds, which is way over the 2.1 second SLA. *What happens next?* Teams typically throw more hardware at the problem, perhaps trying to install more servers, memory, storage, etc. in the test lab. But more often than not, this fails to solve the root problem.

 Elaboration: The performance test team *intends* to invest in technology to better find the issues' root causes. The problem is that that we basically cover up a needle with a huge haystack, then attempt to find the needle. Performance budgeting allows you to find the needle in a very small haystack, inline with any other issue the development team has to resolve.

Fast forward to the "After" example below the timeline, showing how the team decomposed the SLA—giving each piece of the solution its own "performance budget" to tune at the component level. SV allows teams to isolate each of those components by simulating the surrounding dependencies (and the expected or observed response times) of other components in the system.

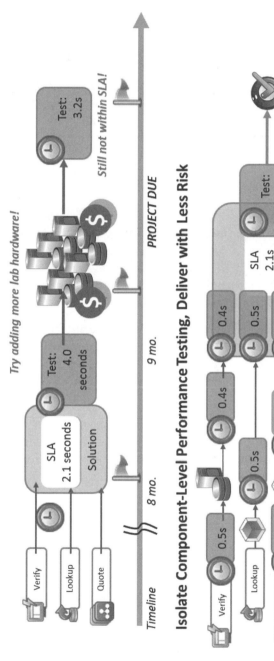

Figure 10-2. Performance budgeting using Service Virtualization. Service Level Agreements (SLAs) typically only require an aggregate response time (shown at top), so traditional performance testing can only guess about the underlying cause of slow performance or recommend more hardware. By decomposing service levels out to individual teams, they can test at a component level in context against Virtual Services and fix underperforming components earlier in development.

Using this method, you can determine, for instance, that the pricing app is delivering excess time to the overall solution. And because you set a budget on the response time, you can individually take corrective steps to tune each component in isolation, faster, and at far lower infrastructure cost.

Informing Performance from Production

In order to keep software projects moving in preproduction, developers and testers make guesses about what happens in production. They might try to guess what users are most commonly doing with an application that is consuming their component's logic, estimate the web traffic on Black Friday, or guess how fast the SAP financials system might respond to a query. The industry of software really needs to innovate and become more scientific here.

Indictment: App development teams are largely uneducated about the actual use and performance of their applications in the product context. They often are wrong when making their "educated" guesses with regard to common use cases, errors encountered, performance profiles, and more. This trend has continued in the wrong direction for a variety of reasons.

With SV, we can capture and simulate the performance and response rate of the back end, as well as measure a profile of the requests that we would typically make of it—the load patterns, scenarios, and types of data we are pushing toward the back end.

When we "shift-left" for quality, we want to do so for performance as well to ensure more reliable outcomes at much lower repair and adjustment costs. SV creates the environment for performance testing, but its response behavior is also informed by system logs and other tools such as load testing and **Application Performance Monitoring (or APM)** tools that can continuously export useful data from production for this profiling (Figure 10-3).

This process is called **Production Data Mining (or PDM)**. A great example would be from a major electronics retailer who was planning to upgrade the Order Management System—from OMS version 2.0 to OMS version 2.1—for their many stores' use for the upcoming holiday season.

Instead of making estimates, let's use SV to capture the performance profile of the underlying systems on an actual business day—the busiest day of the year in fact. Then as we build our new OMS 2.1 release, we can be certain that we are taking into account a range of possible response times (and possibly timeouts) from those systems.

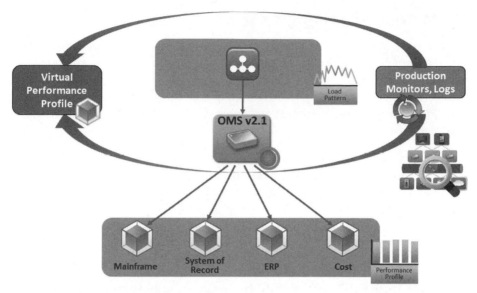

Figure 10-3. Informing Virtual Services from production monitoring allows the performance of Virtual Service response times to be throttled by typical response times that occur in the real-world systems when under certain load conditions. The front-end load can also be similarly captured and profiled for very accurate simulation of traffic for a given time period.

In addition, why not also capture the front end of that scenario, using the observed load pattern from Customer Service requests on that day and feed that data into a load testing solution as a realistic simulation of that front-end interaction? Using PDM with SV provides a real "performance sandwich" around the System Under Development (OMS) we are working on. We gain an early and very efficient way to prove performance of the new system, at a fraction of the infrastructure cost of setting up real environments.

Setting Thresholds to Move Performance Even Farther Left Than We Ever Imagined

There's one more interesting wrinkle we can exploit here, as bottlenecks don't just occur in our own System Under Test (SUT). By observing data of when and how downstream components break or run out of capacity in production, we can set that value in their corresponding VS like a "redline" on your engine, where it goes into the danger zone when pushed too hard. With this behavior in place, you will already know if your application is likely to push a dependency out of its comfort zone and account for it.

Using PDM and SV together to understand performance thresholds allows us to become even more proactive about understanding how to improve end-to-end responsiveness.

Performance Testing by Design

Performance testing has historically never been very agile—because teams could only uncover defects ONE at a time. Basically with each run, performance teams uncover the most significant bottleneck first. Then they would send the application back to development to debug the source of the lag and fix the offending component. Then reset and rerun . . . only to find the next bottleneck and start over again.

Conversely, with SV in place, performance testing is no longer a "big step at the end" at odds with Agile—it becomes an effective enabler for Agile. Now multiple developers and testers as well as the performance lab itself can get their own virtual labs, while collaborating to improve performance within the context of the end-to-end business application.

When we have to make new features, we make assumptions about their performance during design. With component-level performance testing, we can finally do the "R" part of R&D and even make design decisions that we have tested out before they get committed.

Case Study: Performance Testing Takes Flight at Design Time Take our friends at a federal agency. They didn't just conduct performance tests early in development; they used *SV to help make better performance-related choices in design.*

For instance, one aspect of their next release's architecture called for a software messaging technology (an XML Gateway) that would likely handle a lot of traffic. Instead of hoping they could get their vendor's XML Gateway to scale after they invested millions of dollars in and around this critical component, they used Service Virtualization to simulate a basic, but high-capacity environment around it. Then they conducted high volume Non-Functional Testing (NFT), firing transactions against several different vendors' XML Gateway components. The best performing one was then specified for the design—*before a single line of code had been written!*

The same "performance by design" approach also works with external service providers—let's say you are choosing between two transaction processing firms as a SaaS-based back end for your application. You would never have been able to conduct nonfunctional testing this way until now. So don't just wait and see how they perform—set an expectation and validate it!

Best Practice 4: Data Scenario Management

It is not uncommon for some teams to spend fully 40–60 percent of their integration, regression, and performance test cycle times on setting up and cleaning out test data. We've talked about the mess of data issues and the enormous difficulty development and test teams encounter when trying to manage their own projects against an ever-increasing amount of volatile data within out-of-scope systems that are beyond control.

 If you've ever sat on a prerelease conference call with a couple dozen developers and testers at midnight, where a system is reset and everyone waits for the signal to "GO!" to start entering specific test data scenarios into their screen, you already know what we're talking about!

Software teams need to synchronize realistic data scenarios across all systems their apps talk to in the environment to verify business requirements are being met. We call this process "aligning the stars." As our software becomes more distributed and changes faster every day, achieving this level of synchronization becomes practically impossible, and throwing more people at the problem provides little help.

Service Virtualization should be used to bring all of the systems needed into a development and test lab environment, including provisioning the data of out-of-scope systems and maintaining the context of a scenario as it passes between systems in a workflow over time.

vTDM: Just the Data You Need

Just as Service Virtualization has a counterpart in Server Virtualization, there is a mature set of tools for conventional *Test Data Management (or TDM)* that allow you to extract and import data from systems that your teams have been given access to.

But for most development activities in a composite app world, most of the data you need exists in systems that are "out-of-scope" and not under your control. So rather than try to extract data directly from these sources, you should use SV to capture and simulate the behavior of out-of-scope systems by responding with *just enough appropriate data and dynamic behavior to "fool" your system under development into believing it is talking to the real thing*.

We call this *virtual Test Data Management (or vTDM)*.

Using vTDM instead of real TDM seems too simple, but this is actually the healthiest way for your development teams to get stable, relevant test data they can rely on in a lightweight form. SV makes gathering just the data needed from downstream systems much easier by automating the capture of relevant scenarios, intelligently interpreting the kinds of data seen, and masking and manipulating that data as part of a VS.

Virtual Service–based data allows all your teams to always have on-demand access to relevant datasets for systems under test, and that data can be expanded upon to cover almost infinite valid data scenarios to support high-volume performance and regression testing needs.

Eliminate Conflicts over Data

The composite nature of today's business apps lends itself well to dividing development and testing tasks across multiple teams, each with responsibility for their own discrete functionality. This approach can be highly advantageous, if we can apply SV to overcome the scourge of test data conflicts.

Conventional TDM is a very time-consuming process that often concerns several teams, as certain scenarios must be loaded and ready with data coordinated across multiple systems. Once all of this data is synchronized, it can be used to support a given performance or end-to-end test, after which it is "burned" and must be rebuilt before it can be used by anyone again.

Each data setup activity is rather fragile—so if a new release appears in the preproduction stack or another team attempts a test that touches one of the data sources used in a test, it will immediately corrupt the test data, making the results suspect.

Using SV, many of the old conflicts of conventional TDM disappear entirely (Figure 11-1). You no longer need to align the stars to make data appear exactly where you need it, in an appropriate structure and format.

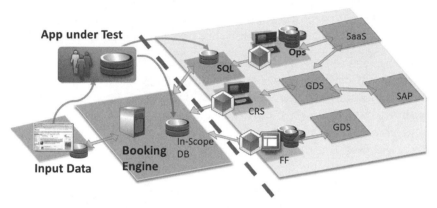

Figure 11-1. Out-of-Scope test data conflicts are addressed by providing each team with all needed scenarios in the form of a Virtual Service that can be launched and run independently of other teams or volatile, changing conditions in the architecture.

Unique situations such as edge conditions, negative test scenarios, and error handling are easily configured in the behavior of the VS, and are never burned since the VS is simply making appropriate behavioral responses. Best of all, each team can always launch their own VS that is already configured and synchronized.

As new software is built, teams use existing vTDM scenarios of downstream systems as the baseline starting point, and then quickly feed in additional scenarios for each new requirement. The resulting updated VS provides documentation for the business cases the team validated, as well as indicates the needed changes for the downstream component. Now when multiple test cycles or teams have differing needs for test data, they will no longer collide in the test lab.

Data Masking: Trust, but Virtualize

Let's touch on one more aspect of vTDM that is always mentioned, especially as we further segment our software development activities across different teams, companies, and even countries: *desensitizing*, de-identifying, or masking test data.*

Many industries have very strict standards about how they handle private customer data—how it is stored, accessed, and transmitted; when and where it needs to be private; and who can see it. For instance, the health care industry in the United States has specific federally mandated controls on how patient data is transmitted and used, such as HIPAA. And data issues for the U.S. Department of Defense are even more extreme.

Even if not mandated by law, all businesses obviously need high standards for data privacy and security to prevent fraud and misuse of that data, or they will pay the consequences in the market. This certainly extends to software development and testing in today's distributed world.

If our company has developers working at our trading partners in Canada and Germany and another large team is doing testing in India, those teams do not need **real** test data with actual customer addresses and ID numbers to do their job. That only matters during a final customer verification process. They only need **valid** test data that supports the needed scenarios and appears in a format that is usable in building their apps and tests.

When employed properly, SV offers a great solution to this problem. Data elements that are captured from live transactions or logs should be recognized, but carefully obscured—we're not talking about "randomizing" responses here, as that only reintroduces the kind of data volatility we are trying to escape!

Take for instance a Visa or MC credit card number. It has a certain format you expect: 16 numbers, starting with a "4" or "5" and other rules. My development teams are fine if the real customer's number is changed to a "fake card number" in this instance, as long as it fits the basic rules and maintains the context of that number throughout their test sessions.

Expected Results

In today's composite apps, the data we need can reside within dozens of different locations, each with its own connection protocols and cryptic formats. Furthermore, much of the live data needed to verify applications and move forward in software projects is sensitive and locked down.

Data scenario management, and finding a better way to do it, has become a really big deal almost everywhere we go. Using vTDM has the potential to save thousands of wasted hours. Since SV at heart is simply "having a conversation" with other systems, harnessing that dialogue for vTDM is a natural fit.

Expected Benefits of virtual Test Data Management:

- Improves overall delivered quality due to more thorough and stable data scenarios

- Eliminates delays due to lack of access or current data from out-of-scope systems

- Provides on-demand availability and faster spinup of valid data scenarios for multiple test and development teams to work in parallel

- Ensures no conflicts over test data or invalidation of other teams' activities by overwriting or changing data in systems

- Has little or no impact on data within critical live systems

- Reduces the time spent on data setups and resets by up to 90 percent, cutting overall lifecycle times by 40–60 percent

Rolling Out Service Virtualization

For us, Service Virtualization is all about the ability to deliver faster, and with higher quality, while reducing our setup time and not having to build new architecture. In our organization, collaboration was key on this initiative. We didn't have a Center of Excellence for this practice, so we had to bring in stakeholders from capacity planning, development, infrastructure teams, as well as functional testing and other groups. It was the first time we really brought all these groups together.

—Laura Miller, VP Global Product Development, First Data Corporation

Achieving a successful adoption of Service Virtualization takes more than getting a current project across the finish line. The best practices of SV become profound change agents when ALL development teams and partners responsible for your software leverage virtual infrastructure to eliminate constraints.

The Stakes for Service Virtualization are Huge, So Don't Settle

SV offers a transformational approach to delivering business technology without constraints. ***Therefore, your goal with SV must be to permanently and substantially improve your company's rate of innovation and return***

on technology investments, now and in the future. Settling for anything less than this transformation is basically conceding the lead to your competition.

But what about the risk? Won't this create upheaval in my organization?

Any time you hear the word "transformation," it sounds risky. But in reality, SV causes very little disruption because it overlays the technology and process you already have. The actual function of SV is to relieve much of the disruption now being caused by change in the software lifecycle.

The reward of faster innovation at lower cost far outweighs any risk. Let's frame SV change in the context of other major IT shifts your company has already made:

- **When you went from mainframe to distributed applications**, you had to change your entire architecture. You brought in new tools and technologies and reoriented your teams from primarily mainframe developers to open and distributed system developers. Instead of owning your whole infrastructure, you started working with services, some of which were managed by other companies. It was an incredibly costly effort, and the results weren't guaranteed. *But going to composite applications was a risk you had to take to get new features to market.*

- **When your company looked at the economics of offshoring,** you saw the potential of realizing a 30 percent or more reduction in labor costs—too compelling a value to ignore. Despite the risk in trusting a remote workforce to get up to speed and deliver critical services, you shifted a significant amount of your labor force from onshore to off. *You took on an enormous risk of business failure and upheaval to obtain this labor efficiency.*

With SV, your company can make a bigger impact on its overall rate of innovation and cost than either of these earlier transformations ever created, without the disruption and without the upheaval. Your EXISTING people should be able to deliver 30 percent or more faster than they do today, with far less investment and time to value. SV is not nearly as hard a pill to swallow, but it can deliver more value at a faster rate than either of these transformations did.

The risk of making the commitment to SV is far outweighed by the reward. *Our goal with SV is nothing less than removing more than half the entire cost of delivering software,* and in so doing, make your company far more agile and innovative in capturing new opportunities.

Changes to the Software Development Lifecycle Process (SDLC)

Leveraging SV does not require a change to your SDLC. In fact, the effect of SV on your overall SDLC is that your processes should execute much closer to your intentions than they likely do now, with far less friction (Table 12-1).

In a traditional SDLC, discontinuous development cycles "crash together" in the system test function, followed by an integration test function, then by performance and user acceptance testing.

Honestly, very little real "testing" is actually performed in most enterprise SDLCs today. These are more furious shakedown activities, compressed as much as possible to meet a deadline. We know this by the lack of functional issues discovered in system test and the number of component-specific issues found much later in UAT.

Table 12-1. Sample process changes to the SDLC due to Service Virtualization are seldom disruptive, as they tend to ease friction and wait time from each phase.

SDLC Phase	Development	System Test	Integration	Performance
Changes due to Service Virtualization	No writing stubs More component-level functional validation	No hardware procurement No collision over test labs	No environment setup/config Automated scenario data ready	No server test region wait Test at 80–95% higher back-end capacities
Not changing	Everything else	Everything else	Everything else	Everything else

Clearly, there are practitioners in your organization who will need to change their own personal steps within the SDLC. For instance, they should stop the up-front work of writing stubs by hand or standing up huge test environments while configuring data at system and integration test time. In that sense, the steps change but the top-down view of your development and delivery process does not.

SV provides an isolated yet live-like environment for doing system test. This causes more realism and therefore more testing to occur, earlier. We have already documented the impact of "shifting quality left" in general and specifically at Sprint (Chapter 8). When the System Test phase successfully executes as it was intended, the overall SDLC runs more as defined and less as a victim of constraints.

Using VSE back ends, better quality is built into each line of code with earlier development testing, system testing environments can stand up instantly and uncover defects much faster, fewer issues make it through integration and UAT testing, and if they do, they are usually far less costly and severe. None of these delivery benefits are disruptions to the SDLC—they are, in fact, everything we hoped for in an ideal process.

Later we will introduce the notion of how SV affects the Enterprise Release paradigm itself (Chapter 15). There, process changes will indeed occur, as we test and release ever-larger architectures in ever-smaller increments. But let's not get ahead of ourselves. There is tremendous value in simply executing on what you have already documented in terms of process by leveraging SV.

Build New Skills and Roles in a Virtual IT World

Constraints are a problem in every industry that relies heavily on software to function. We talked about simulation in other engineering disciplines, but the concept is not entirely without precedent for software. Some financial companies have had a large technical staff doing simulation for a long time— but only for things that are very specific to their industry, such as predictive risk analysis and validating banking protocol standards.

In some telcos, there is literally an entire career track for "simulation engineers"—thousands of developers writing tons of simulation code for system feedback that NEVER sees a customer and NEVER processes a business transaction.

Fast forward to now, and it is particularly interesting to see how companies are defining new job titles and sometimes even new departments for tasks such as building and managing environments. Adjusting titles and departments like this is certainly not a prerequisite of a successful SV initiative, but it does provide an interesting "sign of the times" of what is happening in the field.

Good Help Is Virtually Always in Demand

SV is rapidly becoming an area of focus and continuous improvement for major companies. Therefore, SV is also becoming a highly demanded strategic job skill. Right now, the number of available resources with meaningful experience applying SV in enterprises falls far behind the demand for these developers, architects, and testers.

Closing this SV "talent gap" is not really a question of aggressive recruiting practices. The best adoption of SV grows from within a company. Companies that consistently take on an attitude of mentorship will do the best. Here are some good pointers we've seen for improving SV proficiency:

- **Take the help:** If your software delivery or SI firm can bring experts to the table to deliver services such as training, release strategy, and initial implementation, by all means accept the help! The benefits of a faster rampup and more complete adoption will far exceed the cost.

- **Absorb knowledge:** Wherever the most meaningful SV project activity is happening, put your best people from other groups to "shadow" or work next to that delivery team and get them up to speed fastest.

- **Share often:** Skilled SV practitioners who are good at modeling and simulation should become resources for the rest of the company, for instance by posting examples and answering questions in a Wiki, weekly "lunch-and-learns," or informal webinars to discuss current SV work with other practitioners.

- **Have a SV developers' help desk:** Team members may feel like they are stepping out onto thin ice when first using SV instead of test hardware and stubs. If you assign someone that can provide answers or locate good help as they take those first few steps, whether on-call or managing an issue tracking queue, this will bring up everyone's confidence level.

- **Increase everyone's technical savvy for distributed development:** Don't let developers work in silos, as they should now be able to consider their component role in a larger application context thanks to SV. Developers should also raise the tech ability of QA/Test organization team members by training them on concepts of service-orientation, app development and integration—this will make them better understand the needs of component-level testing.

Each of us personally in our own role should help advance SV and think about how it can fit in and enable automation and efficiency across our entire extended IT organization, including our partners. This includes both "How can I make my job easier with SV?" and "How can I leverage the practice of SV to better involve everyone to achieve the company's value goals?"

Should We Centralize or Federate?

One of the questions we get asked most is this: *"Should I centralize SV within the corporate environment that all teams use, or should we just give out SV to everyone so they can do their own thing?"*

Our answer is that you should have an equilibrium or hybrid of the two approaches (and in this case, the word "hybrid" is not just a cop-out on making a decision). Generally, here's what we recommend:

- **Centralize VS Creation and Catalog:** We want to centralize the administration or ownership of Virtual Services, so usually the initial creation of a VS catalog is assigned to dedicated teams with a high level of expertise and knowledge in this specific skill.

- **Federate for Maintenance:** Here's where it makes the most sense for specific teams of development, test, and performance managers to maintain the Virtual Services. They have a local environment where the maintenance and deployment of their specific vertical or transaction needs occurs.

Often our customers start as centralized and then move to more federated approaches as adoption increases. Let's say we are at a bank that has a central SV Center of Excellence that runs a set of VSEs for the company, and they are quite efficient at making a library of robust Virtual Services at the request of development teams. If this works well enough, why wouldn't we just stick with that centralized format?

The reason you federate VSEs is not just a technical one; rather, it is a part of the Agile mindset we should adopt. We want to federate the use of Virtual Services because we need developers and component teams to take responsibility for **clearing their own constraints** every time they endeavor to deliver a component. To the development team, a centralized VSE is out of their control, capacity constrained, and data restricted. It's great that there is a CoE team leading SV and helping create Virtual Services, but we want developers to be empowered with a real sense of control to move forward faster.

Each team needs to rapidly change their own VS without concern for other teams; they need to be able to bury the VSE server with transaction requests at their own discretion. They also need to be able to completely bring down the VSE for their fault recovery testing needs. If shared use is the only option, it will eliminate all of these possibilities and make the VS team feel no different than any other constrained resource that frustrates teams.

Having the best of both worlds allows SV experts to do the heavy lifting centrally, while developers can go forward and customize their environments to overcome their own specific dependencies without waiting for shared resources.

Cool Alternative Use: Virtual Training Environments?

Here's a very cool new way we have seen both a major telco and a large regional bank employ SV that has NOTHING to do with software development, but still offers a huge value proposition. Let's take the telco for instance. These guys have thousands of representatives, both domestic and offshore, performing different levels of phone, e-mail, and chat-based support functions for customers.

There is a huge amount of accretion or turnover of employees in this function, as it is largely an entry-level role. That means training is a nonstop activity. Like many firms, the old system of training consisted of flying them all into a physical training facility and then giving them a little too much rote instruction and manuals. This was followed by a limited amount of time on terminals in a very costly training environment, with painstakingly mocked-up services, training data, and a training partition on the mainframe—all of which were a huge hassle to set up and maintain for each class—while still being a little outdated compared to the current live software.

Setting up realistic system environments to support training became a nonstop, expensive, back-breaking endeavor. After all, you can't set trainees loose mucking around with real customer data in a live system, but they still needed that "live-like" hands-on experience to learn their jobs.

Using SV, the telco now creates on-demand Virtual Training Environments (VTEs) that contain all the required "safe customer" data scenarios, with the realistic responses and behaviors needed for thorough training (Figure 12-1).

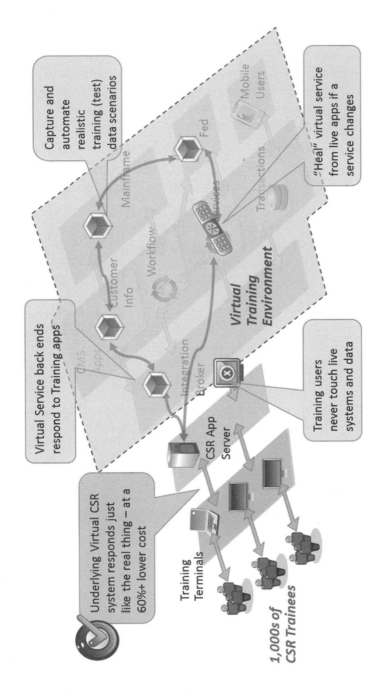

Figure 12-1. Virtual Training Environments (or VTEs) apply the same principles of virtual labs for test and development, except applied to the task of rapidly setting up and provisioning all the back ends and data scenarios needed to support robust employee and partner training, for a higher degree of stability and portability at a fraction of the cost of real environments.

They can instantly launch 100 or 1,000 VTEs behind their educational user interfaces, and even conduct that training remotely through a browser.

So with no more per-user setups, no data scrubbing, unlimited 24/7 access, and the flexibility to deliver that VTE remotely with a high degree of current realism, the firm is better equipping employees to work at a small fraction of the cost. As far as trainees are concerned, they are entering orders and getting appropriate responses from the real back-end systems . . . except maybe faster. (They actually slowed down the Virtual Services a little to make the "wait time" more like the real systems!)

Service Virtualization and DevTest Cloud

"The cloud" may be the most overhyped technology in recent memory. Every major software vendor has jumped on the cloud computing bandwagon. There are good reasons why it captures our imagination. The promise of almost unlimited elastic computing capacity, available in an on-demand, pay-as-you-go model, with management and security aspects of the applications often included for you, is incredibly appealing.

We've seen instances of consumer-oriented startups and SaaS-based business models having success selling cloud-based offerings—most notably Amazon, Salesforce.com, and Apple have gained traction with business models that are a natural fit for cloud. New startups also realize the advantage of cloud infrastructure, as they can basically take a "blank slate" approach to their application design using cloud-based applications, instead of layering on top of existing technology.

So why hasn't cloud caught on for most major enterprise apps? When a larger company attempts to "run business in the cloud," they quickly realize that the well-publicized successes of some cloud business models don't yet translate into enterprise development success for many companies. Cloud has not yet delivered the miracle of pushing critical business software functions to an automatically reusable "app assembly and hosting" environment.

If anything, leaning on cloud-based components to conduct real business in an unplanned fashion will exacerbate development and test constraints and make governance harder. Therefore, enterprises should employ cloud where it makes the most sense—and the *best, first place to leverage cloud is for development and test labs*.

Constraints of Cloud Dev and Test

To do development work in cloud, we will first look for a self-provisioning utility kind of way to stand up and tear down dev and test labs for preproduction.

The setup and provisioning of a real production environment is a huge effort. We are constantly monitoring, maintaining, and managing it carefully to keep it running. Production is so complex and constrained that you are unlikely to ever create more instances of these environments. At the same time, you can't afford to have even a little bit of exposure of these production systems and data to development teams. So by using cloud for development and test, we seek to manipulate that environment more safely in preproduction.

Contrast that big production environment to preproduction use. Dev and test teams need to create and provision new labs EVERY TIME there is an incremental release. There could be hundreds of labs and thousands of conventional VMs of applications that different teams are using (Figure 13-1). Preprod use of virtual labs is where the explosion of cloud is really happening.

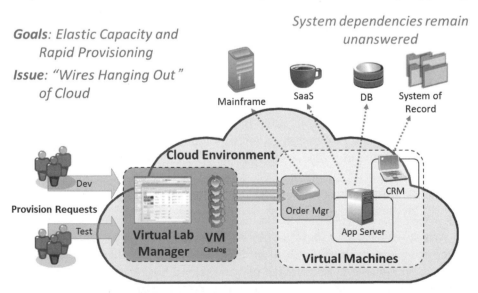

Figure 13-1. "Wires hanging out" of the cloud due to external dependencies for development and test that cannot be imaged or included.

This is great. So what is the problem? There are still "wires hanging out" of your cloud . . .

Let's paraphrase a customer's enlightenment on this issue: *"I tried to move my development and test labs to a cloud to give us that elasticity and let them quickly provision an environment in just minutes—and yes, they can do that quite efficiently for some of our app components. But what about all the "wires hanging out" of our cloud? You can't replicate things like a huge mainframe, copy a third-party fee-based service, or image that huge database in the cloud—yet your development project can't move forward without these elements available. If it takes me three weeks to get access to the mainframe, that means it still takes me three weeks to wait and provision a cloud lab."*

No matter how much you improve the speed of provisioning systems in cloud, you can still only move as fast as your most constrained system allows. Let's instead use Virtual Services to model and represent the off-cloud resources within the same environment (Figure 13-2). No more wires!

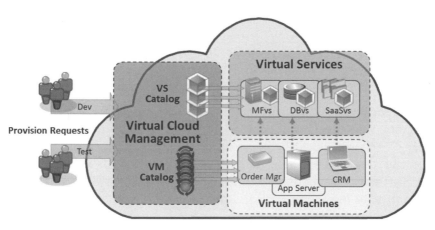

Figure 13-2. No more "wires hanging out of the cloud" with Service Virtualization simulating off-cloud dependencies and data.

Service Virtualization makes cloud real for on-demand development and test environments. You can leverage Virtual Services (VSs) alongside VMs to capture and simulate those "wires hanging out" and manage them in a complete DevTest Cloud environment. Preproduction teams can now get complete labs that include stable versions of all the mainframes, data scenarios, and services they need to truly realize elastic capacity.

Achieving High-Performance Cloud Environments

Cloud is best used when the volatility of demand varies among a variety of uses of a particular infrastructure. Different applications have different capacity

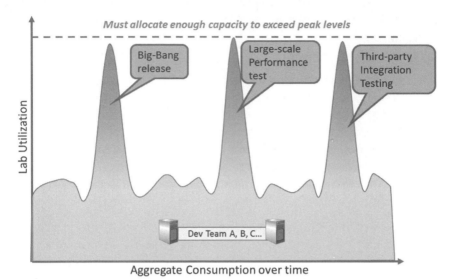

Figure 13-3. Volatile utilization of Performance Lab resources requires the company to reserve enough capacity to handle peak demands, leaving inefficient valleys of lab utilization.

needs over time. The ability to leverage one common resource pool among many teams gives us an appearance of higher capacity on a per-team basis, when in fact we are simply leveraging the unused capacity of other teams.

In the utilization graph shown in Figure 13-3, many teams are leveraging shared infrastructure. One team might peak its usage during performance tuning or a "big bang" release cycle. Other teams are simply doing typical dev and test activities, and they are generating no such peak. This works best if each team plans its peak performance testing times when other teams don't need that additional capacity. In general, it also means we must invest in or reserve the maximum possible capacity.

Using cloud combined with SV allows for a whole new economy in the development of high-performance applications. This creates a dramatic decrease in the cost structure—one effect you can see from Figure 13-4 is that the overall dev and test infrastructure requirements and costs go down for shared capacity, including on-premise and off-premise cloud.

When Virtual Services represent out-of-scope systems, they utilize computing resources far more efficiently than a live system does. For example, it might take several VMs to represent a 25 percent capacity back-end app, whereas a VS will consume only a fraction of the CPU and memory requirements of just one of those machines for preproduction.

In a typical performance test, the entire architecture has to scale to the load desired, making the most over-utilized systems become bottlenecks. In the

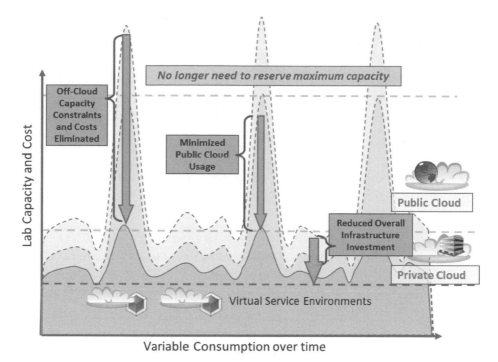

Figure 13-4. Service Virtualization in cloud reduces capacity and cost for development and test performance labs. Peak traffic can be consumed by both private and public cloud capacity if needed, thereby reducing overall spend and still meeting capacity needs.

virtual environment world of VMs and VSs, only the VMs must scale. An almost infinite number of Virtual Services can be instantly launched and utilized on-demand, with all the elasticity the cloud can offer.

If more scale is needed for performance tests, only a fraction of the entire lab must be scaled up, while the typically larger and more complex systems represented by Virtual Services will scarcely need to scale up at all. When an enterprise's IT management team understands their capacity in this regard, they have a greater ability to make sound economic decisions about how to leverage cloud-based infrastructure.

Massively Parallel Regression Testing in Cloud

The desire to perform continuous integration or regression tests on a large scale is not new. Teams have been looking for ways to reduce the time and huge manual effort required for regression testing for years. The use of automation for regression testing is, of course, a well-known way to reduce this time.

However, once a suite of regression tests starts to get very large, test execution again becomes an issue in that the team wants to see the regression results in just a few hours, but the test suites must often run for days.

When pressed for time, how many times has IT had to tell the business, *"You can't get a baby in 4.5 months by adding another mother!"* Well, thanks to SV's lack of capacity constraints, it is time to throw another analogy out the window.

Running a massively parallel test bed requires that your automated testing platform be able to monitor its own execution of tests over time, and dynamically provision additional capacity as Virtual Services into the test bed as needed to reach the time goals provided.

As the tests are running, monitors discover the resource consumption needed to perform the testing and calculate the additional capacity needed to bring the test suite execution into the timeframe desired. As more tests are initiated and staged, more Virtual Service capacity is dynamically added, with all the needed scenarios ready to go.

As you can see in Figure 13-5, the provisioning of SV for massive parallel regression testing in cloud is similar to the elastic capabilities of load and performance testing in cloud. Simply by leveraging testing technology and SV, we can regain the elasticity we expected while taking days off of the average development cycle.

Test Suite 1: Limit to 10 Available Test Servers

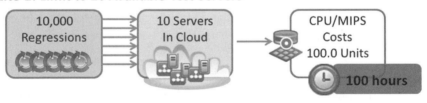

Test Suite 2: Provision Enough Virtual Services to Finish Job in 1 hour

Figure 13-5. Business case for Massively Parallel Regression Testing when using Service Virtualization in cloud. Note that the resource cost when leveraging cloud infrastructure for taking a week to run the test suite and its environment is the same cost for that same test bed to run for just an hour. This is because we generally pay for cloud resources on a consumption basis; hence, if we need 2,000 hours of CPU time we can either do that as 1 machine for 2,000 hours, or 200 machines for 10 hours.

Assessing the Value

The days of accepting multi-year ROI statements from technology providers are gone. In the "new normal," the expectations on IT to deliver faster will only continue to increase, while the economics of application development will remain lean. Therefore, we can't wait to start uncovering value.

Service Virtualization technology benefits are clear and present. It is quite rare for us to see a customer not reach ROI within a few weeks or months of rollout. With full buy-in and mentorship from experts to help make your first implementation successful, **Service Virtualization should pay for itself within a year of your investment.**

As we've discussed, in order for an SV initiative to deliver the most compelling results, value starts with YOU, and your key peers and stakeholders in the organization. Whether you are in management or development, YOU must shift your mindset, and YOU must take on the responsibility to drive results by shifting application development away from depending on physical labs and manually built stubs, toward leveraging automated, dynamic VS environments across the software lifecycle.

Beyond that, the short-term and long-term value your company measures through SV depends on answering two questions:

- *Where did you start as a **baseline**?*
- *What **results** does your company really want most from SV?*

Baselining is a very important activity that must be conducted at the very start of your SV initiative, as you want to base your future results on empirically measured improvements to the current state of software development.

Your team must gather a good baseline at the initiation of SV that not only contains specific numbers, but focuses on results that match the most important IT or software delivery priorities of the company. Without this, you will lack the specific goals you need to *manage* and *incent* SV across your teams—and therefore success will be much harder to demonstrate in your next review.

If we revisit some of those earliest preproject value goals, let's express them as a baseline metric, and then fill them in with the results we measured in the first six months after the start of a successful project.

Table 14-1. Sample of Three Baseline Metrics vs. Results Metrics Typical of an SV Implementation. There are hundreds of possible goals to baseline and measure results from, and monetary values can be assigned to the results depending on the size and accounting methods of the company.

SV Implementation	Faster	Better	Cheaper
Before (Baseline)	Software release happening every 5–6 months	Avg. 5 major, 12 minor defects delivered to QA or Prod	Average 2,500 hours spent on break-fix from Perf team per quarter
After (Results after 6 months)	Software release cycle reduced to 3 months (after 2 cycles)	Only 1 major defect discovered in QA, 6 minor defects	850 hours total spent on break-fix in Q3–Q4

Different IT service providers and software vendors (including our own company's service delivery teams) provide wildly varying methodologies for measuring value. So rather than get into too much detail for a general guide, let's talk about how companies we've seen measure value with SV along the simple lines of realizing "Better, Faster, and Cheaper" software development lifecycles.

Faster: The Value of Time-to-Market

Winning the innovation race is first and foremost about time-to-market. Ask anybody about the most innovative companies in the world and they will immediately mention Apple, Google, or maybe even Dyson (the vacuum cleaner company)—all companies that are consistently fast at delivering new features to market.

Our goals here are to take the air out of the schedule—all that wait time, data reset time, and "slush time" that is set aside for unexpected events and fixes in the project plan. Delivering faster will make you more competitive and agile, and it will certainly shrink your schedule—and with it your labor costs.

Measuring Results: Faster

When we make every hour a productive hour for our teams, labor costs on a per-project or per-feature basis come down dramatically. When we stabilize the environment with SV, we get started faster, gain more reuse out of our work, and automation becomes far more effective. This causes the absolute and relative labor cost associated with every phase of the SDLC to come way down.

Let's look at some examples of metrics we've seen measured by customers in the field in the form of a familiar table, structured as a value scorecard for Faster delivery (Table 14-2):

Table 14-2. Value Scorecard Examples of Faster Delivery through Service Virtualization Sample metrics are drawn from baseline and progress measurements from Service Virtualization client engagements.

SV Scorecard: Faster	Baseline	6 Month	12 Month	Improve-ment
Regression test cycle	92 hours	36 hours	18 hours	80%
Data setup and teardown time	4 days avg	5 hours	4 hours	96%
Per-cycle wait between Sys/Int/ Perf teams	6 weeks	2.5 weeks	3 work days	93%
Release cycle time (overall)	8 months	5 months	3 months	63%

It's easy to estimate the cost of labor hours spent doing particular tasks in a given SDLC, so based on the size of the team involved, a simple cost savings can be generated. But these savings represent just one team, working on one new piece of functionality, for one application.

Most enterprises have hundreds or thousands of applications undergoing change and release cycles today. Therefore, if we are able to multiply these efficiencies across all teams, the value of moving faster becomes a very significant cost savings as well as a huge competitive differentiator.

Indirect Value: Moving Faster

Many companies will only consider the hard-dollar savings or direct revenue increase in their value assessment for lifecycle acceleration with SV. However, there are many indirect value propositions that create very compelling statements:

- **Rate of innovation:** If we are able to deliver releases to market 30 percent faster, can we devote more time to the research and development budget for newer, differentiated features?

- **Revenue uplift:** How much additional revenue would we generate by having this new product or feature ready in 3 months vs. 6–8 months from now?

- **First-mover impact:** If we are first to market, how much market share can we take from our competition?

- **Late-mover compensation:** Conversely, if we are late to market, over time how much market share will we lose by not offering comparable features or services?

- **Time between phases/releases:** Aside from reducing the time required for completing specific project phases, can we continuously reduce days from the lifecycle when the next team expects an early delivery, and is ready to start the next one immediately using virtual environments?

Better: The Value of Quality

Quality can be measured in terms of avoiding the negative impact of poor quality, as well as realizing the positive benefits of good quality. Delivering higher quality to customers is of the utmost importance in a customer-driven economy, yet it is seldom valued as highly as it should be in many organizations.

We know the rate of change and complexity of today's applications increases exponentially every year, making the difficulty and cost of testing and assurance increase with it. Yet many companies squeeze quality out of their timeline by exclusively incenting faster delivery or cost reduction, thereby making testing and performance appear to be a cost center rather than a critical part of the revenue engine.

The most successful software organizations will incentivize quality across the entire SDLC, including test-driven development, functional testing, and performance engineering as highly necessary parts of the software lifecycle and a requirement of successfully delivering product to market.

Results: Better Quality

Many of our customers experience high costs to resolve defects that are released into production, and they know they pay a much higher price today for problems overlooked months ago. SV allows you to dramatically reduce defect counts and capture that savings for more productive uses.

With the proviso that results vary widely with application and development circumstances, let's look at a "better quality" scorecard of sample value measurements (Table 14-3):

Table 14-3. Value Scorecard Examples of Better Quality through Service Virtualization. Sample metrics are drawn from baseline and progress measurements from Service Virtualization client engagements.

SV Scorecard: Better	Baseline	6 Month	12 Month	Improvement
Defects per KLOC from development	300	100	50	83%
Regression test scenarios covered	5%	50%	90%	1,700%
Number of defects referred to break-fix	30	10	5	83%
Customer support issues reported per quarter	2,500	1,500	1,000	60%

Most companies can monetize the hard-dollar value of quality metrics and set a baseline by keeping track of their historical information on the average number of issues, average hours spent on resolution times, and chargebacks for penalties or refunds, both in preproduction and later in production.

We often see a 60 to 80 percent reduction in the number of high-severity defects released to production, as there is more testing being conducted by every team, all the way back to early development. This represents a dramatic reduction in the cost of support issues and infrastructure around supporting break-fix.

Indirect Value: Better

Faster innovation in isolation is only useful for patents and prototypes. If quality can't keep up with the pace of change, innovation actually becomes an unhealthy thing for customers and your business reputation. There are hundreds of ways companies can measure quality, and SV can bring more predictability to the software lifecycle. Here are a few other considerations companies use to measure quality improvements with SV:

- **Customer satisfaction ratings:** Wise companies will prioritize this single metric as much as any balance-sheet figure, as it has the most long-term impact. If the software behind your product or service works flawlessly, customers will be far more likely to recommend it to their friends or peers, and far less likely to leave. While factors such as innovation, price, and service play into customer satisfaction, it is very much a quality-driven metric.

- **Service Level maintenance:** Service interruptions or system lags can be extremely costly in terms of missed revenue, as well as possible penalties for nonperformance if SLAs are not met.

- **Ability to offer guarantees:** The converse of SLAs is the company's own ability to predictably offer guarantees of high performance and availability.

- **Partner quality:** This is a huge success factor for companies with an ecosystem of technology and delivery partners. By offering key partners readily available VSEs, they can much more easily validate their own software interactions with your business on a continuous basis, often at much lower cost.

- **Ensuring compliance:** This is a "must-do" priority that drives many companies facing government and industry regulations. SV is critical for providing a reference system for certification of quality levels, while supporting the requirements of data masking or privacy, security of critical live systems, and more.

Cheaper: The Value of Cost Savings

The third value of *cheaper* development is almost always the very first one measured by companies concerned with infrastructure savings. With each new release, each new partner, and each new technology we introduce into our environment, the associated software infrastructure and service costs will almost always continue to increase faster over time. We are not only building new functionality—we have to verify that it works against all the old systems. Therefore, even if hardware and bandwidth become cheaper to buy, infrastructure costs will still rise drastically when left unchecked.

Infrastructure cost savings vary wildly from a drip of reducing incremental costs by hundreds of thousands of dollars a month to saving tens of millions in one shot. That savings function has more to do with your current investment level, your planned investment level, and the amount you leverage SV to reduce third-party costs and deliver additional capacity in the performance lab.

Results: Cheaper (Lower Costs)

Aside from labor hours saved, reduced infrastructure is the easiest cost savings to quantify—as you have very specific ideas of your current spending. You likely have already budgeted what you will probably spend on environments, plus you can identify how much infrastructure you can more efficiently manage or repurpose.

Let's look at a sample scorecard for "Cheaper" value measurement of infrastructure and other cost savings (Table 14-4):

Table 14-4. Value Scorecard Examples of Cheaper Development Infrastructure through Service Virtualization. Sample metrics are drawn from baseline and progress measurements from SV client engagements.

SV Scorecard: Cheaper	Baseline	6 Month	12 Month	Improve-ment
Number of test servers in preprod environment	60	30	10	83%
Mainframe partitions needed	13/max charges	6/ unlimited	4	69%
Licensing and config costs for development environments	$15M	$10M	$5M	67%
Third-party partner fees for preprod service access	$700K/month	$150K	$0K	100%

Even if a conventional dev and test lab strategy only delivers 10 percent of the sizing of live environments, this represents a ton of infrastructure, with very high licensing, configuration, and capacity charges. Every lab you currently construct today must have a full complement of components, capacity on shared services, and manually built stubs and workarounds.

When you think about all of the plans for new infrastructure on the table, as well as the unplanned investments that we can avoid, you will be amazed at the hard dollars you can redirect to innovation and more productive activities with SV—and the infrastructure footprint of the SV version will be one to two orders of magnitude smaller.

In addition to its dramatic infrastructure savings, SV enables performance labs to do production-level load at a much higher frequency, with no additional MIPS charges.

Indirect Value: Cheaper

There's an interesting development worth mentioning here, as we are seeing many firms concerned about *cost structure* *in addition to cost savings*. Especially with the infusion of cloud, lots of teams are trying to turn infrastructure purchases and even applications into subscriptions. These companies are seeking to eliminate any expected *CapEx* for IT infrastructure and convert that cost to *OpEx*—and thereby pay a recurring fee to another company or partner to manage the infrastructure externally.

While this may appear to be shuffling costs around in a sense, it is more desirable for some companies' accounting practices to be a renter of infrastructure, rather than having assets tied up as an owner. However, the benefits of this switch are tempered if unexpected lab costs in that "rented" infrastructure cause significant problems with preproduction activities. SV can provide a great insurance policy against preproduction infrastructure costs getting out of control.

For example, a leading transport company we worked with switched to cloud infrastructure and managed application vendors wherever possible in its production environments, but reduced its vendor spend for test labs and partitions—as they could more reliably simulate those environments using SV with no fees.

Additional Indirect Values of Cheaper Infrastructure

- **Major re-architecture cost avoidance:** We mentioned that many companies won't count "cost avoidance" as a real IT cost savings, but when application projects fall behind and problems truly become critical, they must either spend heavily to re-architect the development and test environment or try another way with SV.

- **Better collaboration:** The ready availability of virtual environments eliminates conflicts over shared and live systems in preproduction, as well as aligning all teams and partners for more productivity thanks to less finger-pointing and dependency.

- **Avoid service and VM "sprawl":** Many companies find that they attempt to reduce excess Intel boxes in the server room, only to find that they are rapidly proliferating a huge mass of VMs and preproduction services across teams that are even more difficult to manage and govern. By comparison, SV provides "easy come, easy go" assets. Though a given VS can be highly valid and intelligent, it requires little or no upkeep and helps reduce this clutter and cost.

- **Incentive to test early and often:** This feeds back to better quality, but since infrastructure for test in preproduction is generally seen as a cost and not a revenue generator, this discourages teams from testing as early or often as they should. If teams can afford that infrastructure at a low cost of entry and incremental cost, the impact on delivery efficiency and effectiveness will be huge.

Organizational Roadmap: Planning to Continually Improve

Do you notice a trend in the preceding value measurements? Just like our applications, they are never standalone. They are highly interconnected and cumulative—so results in one area will create increasing value in others.

If you think about it in the broadest sense, *Service Virtualization basically provides decision support for the IT investments of the organization.* SV gives anyone who needs to build, use, or manage software capabilities in your business a more meaningful way of predicting "what if" results for any change in technology direction that happens, so the company can become more agile with less risk.

*For instance, if I automate with SV and decrease the time spent managing stubs and test data, that makes my regression cycle much **faster**. This also allows teams to have ready environments to build and run more test scenarios and increase coverage,* *which makes the software **better** quality. That quality also reduces the hours spent fixing software as well as buying additional infrastructure in the break-fix lab, so the software is far **cheaper** to build and support. Then I can take that two weeks' time to make design-level R&D choices that could make software **faster** to deliver for a new set of customers and so on, and so on . . .*

Most companies conduct value assessments annually after adoption, with reviews at the 6-month, 12-month, 24-month, 36-month mark, and so on. Tracking value at a lower frequency often means the company isn't serious about the results, and is still thinking of SV as a "tool" to complete a given project.

We can look at the balance sheet of a company that is just 2 percent better in a key investment metric like *R&D spend vs. Services revenue*. Comparing these numbers with peers in the industry can speak volumes about the priorities of the company. The IT shop may THINK they are efficient by looking at some bottom-up successes, but in reality they will not stack up as well as they hoped with competition. The corporation has to think about the balance sheet from the top-down and use IT investments to reflect long-term value.

Will your organizational roadmap encourage success? Or inhibit it?

An **organizational roadmap** is a rolling plan that sets the future goals for adoption and collaboration, based on the long-term results of SV in terms of the bigger picture of the enterprise, its market, and its competition.

The importance of a strategic approach increases along with the size of the enterprise, and its overall opportunity for making gains. If you are building and releasing some VS assets on an ad-hoc basis for a product division, you might still measure a couple million dollars in value just by reducing hours and eliminating some service costs . . .

But let's say your goal is to squeeze more than *$100 million or $200 million* out of the entire IT budget over the next year—not unreasonable at all for some global companies.

If your company intends to realize these bigger goals, you had better create an organizational roadmap to achieve that level of continuous improvement, including everything from training and mentorship to communication plans to roles and responsibilities—all the way to execution. Real line items for SV activities should be propagated into every upcoming software development and integration project.

Conclusion

Paris. December 28, 1895. An audience
takes their seats in Le Salon Indien du Grand
Café, paying a franc each to view the first
ever publicly projected film, "Train Pulling Into
a Station." The pioneering brothers Lumière
dim the lights, and a moving picture of less
than a minute in length begins, opening with
a shot of passengers waiting at Marseilles La
Ciotat Station. As a locomotive began to roll closer in the shot, the audience
immediately jumps from their seats, scrambling to the exits in fear for their lives.

Scary, huh? It's kind of funny when you think about this story, but are normally reasonable managers and developers committing the same gaffe today with Service Virtualization? More than 100 years ago, an audience saw the room was empty, and they sat down in front of a screen to witness a new technology. While they might have cognitively known it wasn't real, they still instinctively feared the train.

While we find this old tale amusing, we also see it as a parallel of any truly disruptive technology—especially one like SV. Even if development and performance teams learn about all the advantages of SV, **when it comes down to the next big project, they instinctively fear moving forward without the real systems.**

We were recently at a regional SV industry forum where an SVP of Development for a large entertainment firm talked about the fact that, based upon the cost savings, his office was going to require ALL the firm's development and test teams to use ONLY Virtual Service environments instead of real servers and VM images by one year out.

To which one development director instinctively blurted, *"Wait, that's fine for the Services team, but it's not going to work for us—for our project we still need access to the live integration server, and all the data we need to test the scenarios."* He was OK with other teams using SV, but afraid to step out of the real world on his own—so afraid in fact that he had to contradict his boss right there in the meeting!

The SVP didn't miss a beat after the interjection: *"We actually switched your team's environment over to Virtual Service back ends first about six months ago—you've been developing against them ever since. Did you notice anything different?"*

Hey, we hear this everywhere we go, and we can understand the guy's trepidation about stepping off the real platform into something virtual, into something he's never known. Just like those folks seeing the train virtually bearing down on them in 1895, we should know that SV isn't scary. But we instinctively fear the unknown and worry about what will happen on our next big project if we don't have the real system—when in fact SV is far less scary than using the real thing.

SV is inherently far more stable, predictably available, safe, and inexpensive than using production-style environments and live data.

The Industrialized Software Supply Chain

As enterprise software developers and managers, we accepted the reality of constraints in our work for years as well. And we accepted that we'd forever use manual mocks and workarounds just to try and get the job done. Therefore, it is completely understandable if the idea of dispensing with them entirely seems too good to be true.

Having read this book to this point, you know how SV is the productization of the old practice of stubbing and mocking throughout the software development and test lifecycle.

SV lets us industrialize the modern supply chain for software to keep up with today's demand, from simulation in design, through assembly and optimized delivery. This should make a huge impact someday . . .

But then you will return to work on Monday and begin planning for the next big, critical software integration and release project—that all-important new "wing" on your airplane. And your development teams (or "wing designers") will say, *"Great! Where are my 20 real airplanes?"*

 You aren't going to win the innovation game if you only use SV on your least critical projects. You have to be willing to change your thinking before you can change anyone else's thinking. You have to sign up for the science of simulation, and sign up for total predictability throughout your SDLC. Nothing less will do if you want to outpace your competition.

There will come a time that you, your team, and your entire organization, will say, *"We MUST use a Virtual Service instead of a live system—because it is the ONLY way we can actually control our environment and predict our ability to deliver."*

Other industries have achieved great efficiencies through simulation. So why haven't we done so in software development? If you asked an engineer at Boeing to build a wing design now without modeling and simulation, they would tell you, *"No way. I need a wind tunnel and modeling software, not a plane!"*

It's not like we just made up this idea as an invention—we saw that other industries and systems already know there is no way to develop complex things like this without simulation technology. Simulation needs to be pervasive, it needs to be easy, and it needs to be par for the course!

So the next time you have a project start, tell your developers, *"Sorry, but you will NOT use production-style labs, not anymore. Use Service Virtualization instead. I know it is scary, but you will find it is far faster and more predictable than the real servers."*

Innovate and Thrive in Good Times and Bad

SV is mandatory in both good times and bad. I'm going to use our friends down under in Australia to demonstrate this concept, as many of the most successful enterprise adoptions of SV have happened there.

When times are GOOD, businesses demand faster time-to-market and more aggressive software delivery schedules to capitalize on ideal conditions. For instance, while the rest of the world was feeling an economic pinch starting in 2008, Australia had strong resources and a growing economy. Therefore, they needed *unconstrained development* to seize on business opportunities in Asia and the rest of the world.

A small company gets better and bigger by being aggressive with its IT investments in good times. That's why you began to see virtually every bank in Australia as well as other IT-enabled companies radically accelerating their development shops by adopting VS environments, and even deploying them in development clouds in recent years.

But what about bad economic times? We are familiar with a different reality for the last few years in North America and Europe. Overall budget slashes and IT cost-cutting measures happened across the economy. Yet many companies still invested in SV when times were bad. Why?

Increasing IT efficiency in bad times with SV allows companies to keep their existing developers making gains in productivity, helps their systems adjust more quickly to the impact of meeting new regulations, reduces costly defects, retains loyal customers with better services, and reduces the infrastructure and operating cost of software.

Companies usually grow in good times, but they grow relative to each other even faster during BAD times. The companies that can deliver on their promises while maintaining high quality will retain customers, and further, those that can innovate through hard times will gain new customers and come out ahead when good times return.

Prepare to Revisit Your Enterprise Release Strategy

Let's look at a story well-known by anyone in e-commerce and retail. Let's say you accept credit cards on your site and connecting to that company's system accounts for a huge portion of your customer transactions. You get a notice of an upcoming major upgrade at the credit card company, and soon after, access to a "test system" version of the new vendor network release that has certain limitations on traffic. You are only 45 DAYS from go-live. Your enterprise is now in a mad dash to adjust and test your own apps in less than 45 days, or your core business is in huge trouble.

But here's the rub: *many of these changes were known months ahead of time by the credit card company*—they just weren't implemented yet. Instead of having to wait to deliver a finished test environment, their thousands of customers could have been given *three to four more months* to do their critical adjustments to their apps, if the credit card provider had only delivered a Virtual Service based on all the known requirements and API changes to date. Just like defining the "bank in a box" that our "Virtual Poster Child" talks about in the Afterword.

This kind of story is not isolated. It happens in every extended enterprise
. . .

Enterprise-wide coordination was not demanded years ago. Application teams were their own islands; they enjoyed mostly independent architectures, and therefore did not have to synchronize changes with other applications. *Oh for those simpler days . . .*

Today's organizations aiming for the highest levels of cost avoidance, increased agility, and top-line revenue impact have targeted optimizing their entire **Enterprise Release** strategy. You know, the "big bang" release that drives everyone into an annual frenzy.

By using SV across organizations and teams, they concurrently run several development teams in parallel, then bring those many development teams into one integration and test environment for a coordinated release to production.

But wait—Enterprise Releases might be the single most anti-Agile process change we could possibly have adopted! How many times will our development teams be able to deliver a business-critical change in a few weeks—while the next release train won't be available for many months? Our agility disappears when we force coordination among dozens of applications that aren't even involved in the task at hand to get each app change delivered.

In time, even the largest organizations will find that many steps of an Enterprise Release can be optimized away with the effective use of Virtual Services. We already showed you an example of a compressed Enterprise Release plan in a telco case study. The next logical step is to enable many more application changes to occur outside the Enterprise Release schedule with pairwise integration testing, instead of building out an entire integration/test landscape for each team (Figure 15-1).

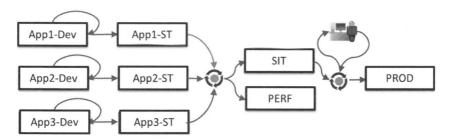

Figure 15-1. A high-level view of synchronized continuous release cycles across multiple teams contributing to a larger Enterprise Release process with Service Virtualization.

Ultimately, we are convinced that by using SV even wholesale enhancements to your applications will be safely delivered to production—without requiring massive coordination efforts among applications and teams that shouldn't even need to be involved.

Chapter 15 | Conclusion

How many times in your career have you been asked to "get real"? How often have real-world boundaries crushed your best ideas? We happen to believe that Service Virtualization can indeed reset your expectations of reality, at least in the realm of software innovation.

True, this one book won't let you escape the world's business limitations. But we hope it has given you a little mental break from reality—the kind of self-delusion we could all use to fine-tune our capacity for innovation. Success was right there for the faking all along. After all, ***reality is overrated.***

Virtual Confession

From the Desk of a Service Virtualization Poster Child

I guess you could say I was the guy they invented Service Virtualization for.

Back in 2007 I was SVP of IT performance and resiliency at one of the top banks in the world. But I wasn't on top of the world. Like most peers in my position at other companies, I had a constant volcano brewing on the application surface of a business that needed to handle several billion transactions a day.

To compete, we needed to keep delivering new features to our customers through our website, teller and ATM networks, and mobile devices—and have them perform flawlessly. But unfortunately, most of the things we needed to ensure that this actually happened were either moving targets or beyond my control.

For any new release, we had to verify that the software our teams built would work in a production environment against more than 200 back-end systems, from mainframes to data stores, as well as systems acquired from other companies, and services hosted by other parties for things like credit checks and transfers. Simply getting all of these systems aligned could happen maybe once a month, and the setup process and fees cost millions of dollars per release cycle. Most of these systems were too heavy or out-of-scope for us to possibly virtualize conventionally as a VM. We had a large team of consultants trying to code our own "responders" to answer this challenge.

Obviously these stubs weren't good enough representations of a complex and changing environment. Projects often ran 50 percent or more past deadline, as critical problems were popping up near the end of each release cycle. We were in fact so constrained that I had a $30 million+ infrastructure purchase order sitting on my desk to try and build an appropriate scale version of production that we could use.

When John Michelsen first showed up in our office and told me about Service Virtualization technology I thought "This has got to be a joke! You can't do that!" I had gotten so used to the constraints of system unavailability, and the manual effort of mocking up services and data, that it seemed impossible.

But this new type of virtualization worked for real. In two weeks, we were able to create a Virtual Services environment for 70 back-end systems and complete an integration-level performance test with it, something we couldn't accomplish reliably with 25 people custom coding for two years on our own. We avoided cutting that $30 million+ check, and I estimate we have missed at least three more of those size infrastructure outlays over the last three years.

But the biggest impact of SV happened when we spread its use across the larger enterprise.

We were able to design a reusable resource we called a "bank in a box"— which required that any team or partner wanting to deliver a new release into our environment actually certified that their code worked at the level expected in our "virtual world" before getting released into our QA and production environments. This made a huge impact on delivered quality and timelines—as well as getting back the nights and weekends we once spent putting out fires.

I can't estimate the value we created with Service Virtualization now in terms of revenue uplift due to an average 35 percent faster time-to-market—we actually stopped trying to measure ROI after year 1 but it is well over $100 million. The agility we gained from simulating real-world IT environments, 24/7, on-demand, for use by hundreds of development, partner and test teams had a huge impact on an entire organization's ability to deliver new features for customers. Better, faster and cheaper than our competition.

I invite you to join the discussion, and learn about the practices and technology behind Service Virtualization. While it is an emerging discipline, SV is now supported by several major consulting and software vendors, and I have had the pleasure of growing this practice across many different groups within a global enterprise for more than five years, and now taking it out to other companies.

Every day I hear about new ways customers in other industries are using SV to optimize their overall delivery capabilities. You don't need to be an engineer to see the business value of having everything in your IT environment ready when you need it.

Virtually Yours,

An IT Executive

Glossary

Agile methodology. Practice of empowering smaller software development teams of requirements owners and developers to define, code, and test functionality in smaller increments, rather than in a large, sequential or *Waterfall* (q.v.) approach.

big data. Data sets that have become too complex, unstructured, distributed or cumbersomely large in size (often measured in petabytes or exabytes) to be managed within conventional relational database systems. As big data can be stored across several systems, it often needs to be managed and referenced differently, using massively parallel systems and new technologies to leverage it.

build. The step of compiling and assembling the code and/or components of a given piece of software, prior to testing/validation in pre-production, or runtime in production. Usually handled by a tool such as ANT or within the software team's ALM (Application Lifecycle Management) solution of choice.

capital expense (CapEx). Accounting term for business spending related to increasing capital, or the means for producing goods, including new equipment, hiring workers, facility construction, software licenses, etc.

Center of Excellence (CoE). A department or organization within a larger enterprise that maintains a centralized embodiment of training, best practices, and implementation aids for the larger organization on a particular topic.

CICS. A form of transaction management software that runs on the mainframe produced by IBM. Many CICS customers' enterprise software eventually has to "talk to CICS" at some point behind the scenes of web applications and integration layers for execution.

client/server. Early definition of any distributed software architecture, involving a "client" system that makes requests of a "server" system that either retrieves or processes data and makes a response to the client. Client/Server came about as a next step in evolution atop mainframe computers in the '80s and '90s when desktop PCs became popular clients for business software.

composite applications. For purposes of this book, we describe "composite apps" as the next level of advancement in today's distributed software architecture. While the first defined *Client/Server* (q.v.) environments may have only included two or three layers of system architecture, composite applications generally contain three, four, or many more tiers and often horizontal integration among applications.

constraints. Anything that hinders progress or completion of a task; a hindrance to throughput or limitation of capacity. Specifically in business terms, we are referring to *constraints* as bottlenecks in the supply chain of software development and delivery, à la Eli Goldratt's *Theory of Constraints*. Look that one up when you have more time.

continuous integration (or CI). Software development practice of more frequent unit and regression testing, and faster check-in of any changes developers make to application code, in order to avoid additional integration problems that happen because the other features of the application have changed while that developer was working on the source code.

desensitizing. Method of obscuring, obfuscating, or otherwise masking private data such that it is de-identified from the original private data usually for the purpose of development and test environment use of the data. This prevents unauthorized viewers from seeing the private data of real users (like user passwords, SSNs, and addresses).

Enterprise Application Integration (EAI). A form of distributed architecture that involves multiple types of business applications as components, for instance a CRM sales application, a financials system, and a pricing/configuration application. Often these systems are provided by different specialized business software vendors.

Enterprise Release. A strategy for implementing large-scale changes to one or more *composite applications* (q.v.) by coordinating the parallel development and synchronized testing and promotion to production of the usually widespread set of changes implemented.

Enterprise Service Bus (ESB). An integration backbone middleware solution that allows disparate software components to be connected by handling and routing message traffic between them—for example, transporting messages between a web service call and an underlying Java app, Oracle database, or SAP Financials system.

Extreme Programming (XP). A form of *Agile* (q.v.) software development methodology that is without irony "taken to extremes," including very rapid development and release timeboxing, development in paired developer teams, and more.

Gantt chart. Typical diagram for business project management, showing tasks and resources along a horizontal timeline, including dependencies and milestones for completion.

hypervisor. A software platform that can run and manage several conventional *Virtual Machines or VMs* (q.v.) of imaged hardware or desktop OS images for higher efficiency of *under-utilized* (q.v.) IT resources.

in-scope. Systems and the data associated with those systems that are within the responsibility purview of a given application development or testing team.

IT governance. Process for aligning a company's IT strategy with their business strategy, or in other words, aligning the priorities for IT around specific business outcomes, and putting the organizational controls in place to do so.

mainframe. Core back-end IT computing platform that is among the oldest architecture still in use; typically handles high volumes of critical transactions and necessary operations. Also called "Big Iron" to denote large scale (and often large footprint) in the data center.

mock or stub services. Software routines that are manually coded to respond to a test request with a piece of data. While stubs are usually rather simplistic and supply rote answers to requests, some development teams invest significant amounts of time trying to code and maintain hundreds of these routines to increase the fidelity of their application testing.

Moore's law. This maxim notes that hardware computing power, in terms of processing speed and capacity, increases exponentially over time, generally doubling every year. (That's fortunate, because the world's need for computing power and data storage is also increasing exponentially.)

new normal. Any current reality that requires a long-term shift in expectations and behavior. In terms of this book, the New Normal represents the fact that businesses expect ever greater functionality to be delivered by IT departments, but the commensurate increase in IT budgets is not happening.

non-relational. A data source that does not hew to relational database standards. This is becoming more common recently as Internet-based applications continue to grow in scope and distribution across multiple components or locations. In a non-relational data scenario, there is no conformity of the data to so-called normalized columns of data types and rows of data instances, and multiple data stores may have redundant or different local data. The forgoing of these tight relationships is built into the expected behavior of the application that leverages such sources (see Big Data).

operational expense (OpEx). Business accounting term for any recurring expenditures that enable the ongoing operations of the business, often including rent, power and other utilities, payroll service, security, network fees, etc.

out-of-scope. Any downstream or upstream systems or data that are not within the control or authority of a given application development and testing team. These may be live systems that are off-limits at times, or resources that are managed by other departments or even business partners.

over-utilized. When a system is frequently accessed by users such that the shared usage impacts the effectiveness of the system for those users.

Profit and Loss (P&L). Business accounting term denoting an individual manager or department's responsibility for achieving certain measured fiscal performance goals, i.e., revenue vs. expenses over a given quarter or period of time.

Relational Database Management System (RDBMS). Type of database that is largely an industry standard today, which stores both data and the relationships among that data in tables. Most DB2, Oracle, SQL, and JDBC-compliant databases are RDBMS.

Rich Internet Application (RIA). A web application where much of the presentation logic and behavior is presented within the browser, using any number of browser plug-ins or presentation technologies (HTML5, Flash/Flex, Java Swing, etc.) to provide a "richness" of user experience. One interesting aspect of RIAs for more complex business functionality. they may make dozens or hundreds of individual calls to back end systems in order to represent that dynamic app in a browser, making good integration quality and performance even more important.

scrum. An *Agile* (q.v.) software development method for precisely timed development and delivery steps, with frequent progress feedback to allow projects to remain malleable to business requirements, especially in situations where there is not a lot of central control or authority defining specific software requirements up front.

Server Virtualization (aka Hardware Virtualization aka OS Virtualization). Technique of creating a software-only image of a given piece of hardware, including the processor, hard drive and possibly the OS or programs running on that hardware, as a *Virtual Machine or VM* (q.v.), which is a more lightweight asset that can be run with other VM images in an environment called a *hypervisor* (q.v.).

Service Level Agreement (SLA). Contractual requirements with a business entity that represents the expected performance and reliability levels of any delivered application. Often an SLA is expressed as a certain speed of response time, or a guarantee of scalability and availability up to a certain predetermined set of circumstances.

Service-Oriented Architecture (SOA). A model for building composite applications that are highly distributed and componentized into smaller, reusable software components that are loosely coupled, with the intent of allowing greater flexibility and reuse from these components to more quickly adapt to meet business requirements. Often involves Web Services (WSDL/SOAP) layers, but SOA can be accomplished using many other integration and messaging technologies.

Service Virtualization (SV). Read this book.

Software Development Life Cycle (SDLC). The entire process of designing, developing, testing, and releasing any software product or project.

sprint. A short window of time, usually less than a month, in which a small gathering of developers focuses on delivering a specific next set of functionality for a software application. A tenet of *scrum* (q.v.) as well as overall *Agile* (q.v.) methodology.

stateful. Data that maintains its context across a software workflow as it passes through multiple decision points or steps in a given process. It is especially important to have stateful logic in *Virtual Services* (q.v.) that must simulate a complex business transaction with variables such as dates/times, cumulative balances, etc. that should remain in lock-step with the intended functional or performance use case. For instance, if I am making and checking airplane reservations over a 24-hour period today and tomorrow, a flight that is available this evening should be stateful enough to know it should be expired tomorrow when it receives a similar request.

stateless. Data or application behaviors that do not maintain the user's context within the workflow of an application over the course of several transactions. Generally this means a given request will get the same response from a stateless stub or service regardless of previous requests that the requestor has made.

Test Data Management (TDM). A system that manages the import, conditioning, setup and teardown of data within a testing environment, usually within databases or systems that are in-scope. Most TDM solutions are designed for heavy lifting types of data extraction and porting in the final verification stages of testing, rather than simulating very "lightweight data" models as seen in virtual services.

Test-Driven Development (TDD). Agile-related software development methodology of first defining a unit test for an expected functionality, before development of that functionality starts. When the test passes, the functionality is then considered complete.

under-utilized. Systems that seldom, if ever, run at capacity. This describes most physical infrastructure and servers in an IT shop, but under-utilization can usually be easily remedied using conventional *Server Virtualization* (q.v.) and *VMs* (q.v.), or many other methods.

Uniform Description, Discovery & Integration (UDDI). Proposed standard for having a directory of Services that can be located within a distributed architecture, and using that UDDI directory to help speed up integration of services and components to build an application.

User Acceptance Testing (UAT). Last-mile testing of an application on behalf of its intended business users and stakeholders at the end of a project, usually conducted exclusively through the application's UI.

virtualization. The general practice of simulating any IT resource, including servers, other applications, networks, devices, and more.

Virtual Machine (VM). A direct image or copy of a given system using conventional or Server Virtualization. Multiple VMs can be managed and run in a *hypervisor* (q.v.).

Virtual Service (VS). An executable model of a given system's behavior usually based on automated observations about messages passing from and to a system under development or test. *Service Virtualization* is the practice of making Virtual Services, and they are run in *VSEs* (q.v.).

Virtual Service Environment (VSE). A management platform that can run multiple *Virtual Service* (q.v.) instances for purposes of interacting with other software components during development and testing. A VSE is the Service Virtualization counterpart to the hypervisor of conventional Server Virtualization technology.

Waterfall development. Traditional serial project approach to software development, involving sequential and ordered phases of development and testing, requiring completion of each step before commencing the next phase. A significant difference in approach from *Agile* (q.v.) in that it attempts to fully pre-define the requirements prior to development commencing, so ongoing changes to those requirements during development are harder to accommodate.

XP. See ***Extreme Programming.***

The journey toward Service Virtualization doesn't stop here.

Join the authors, as well as leading enterprise development managers and IT executives, in the site dedicated to Service Virtualization. Hear case studies and learn more about the best practices and technology that enable SV at ServiceVirtualization.com—your community resource for expert insight and collaboration in a virtual development world!

http://www.servicevirtualization.com

Index